Literature and WAR

Literature
and WAR

CONVERSATIONS WITH ISRAELI
AND PALESTINIAN WRITERS

Runo Isaksen
translated by Kari Dickson

OLIVE
BRANCH
PRESS

An imprint of Interlink Publishing Group, Inc.
www.interlinkbooks.com

First published in 2009 by

OLIVE BRANCH PRESS
An imprint of Interlink Publishing Group, Inc.
46 Crosby Street, Northampton, Massachusetts 01060
www.interlinkbooks.com

This translation has been published with the support of NORLA.

Library of Congress Cataloging-in-Publication Data
Isaksen, Runo.
[Litteratur i krig. English]
Literature and war : conversations with Israeli and Palestinian writers / by Runo Isaksen ;
translated by Kari Dickson. — 1st American ed.
p. cm.
Includes bibliographical references.
ISBN 978-1-56656-730-5 (pbk.)
1. Arab–Israeli conflict—1993– 2. Arab–Israeli conflict—Literature and the conflict.
3. Authors, Israeli—21st century—Interviews. 4. Palestinian Arab authors—21st
century—Interviews. 5. Arab–Israeli conflict—Personal narratives, Jewish. 6. Arab–
Israeli conflict—Personal narratives, Palestinian Arab. I. Title.
DS119.76.I7313 2008
956.9405'4—dc22
2008030373

Cover image by George Azar

Printed and bound in the United States of America

To request our complete 40-page full-color catalog, please call us toll free at
1-800-238-LINK, visit our website at www.interlinkbooks.com, or write to
Interlink Publishing, 46 Crosby Street, Northampton, MA 01060
e-mail: info@interlinkbooks.com

Table of Contents

Introduction

In March 2000, a furious debate raged in Israel, and right-wing politicians in the Knesset threatened the ruling Barak government with a vote of no confidence.

What was all the fuss about? Well, it was about a small piece of literature: a poem. The Palestinian poet Mahmoud Darwish was to be introduced into the school curriculum in Israel on the initiative of the then minister of education, Yossi Sarid, who gave the following explanation for his choice: "It is very important to know one another. Ignorance is not the best recipe for good neighborliness."

Darwish himself was astounded by the whole affair: "It is hard to believe that the strongest military power in the Middle East should feel threatened by a poem," he said. "The first step towards real peace must be to get to know the other side, its culture and creativity."[1]

This book is not about politics—at least, not in the narrowest sense. It evolved from my own experience of reading page upon page about the Middle East, year in and year out, one moment full of hope and the next filled with despair, muttering to myself: "There will never be peace in the Middle East!" And if anyone had asked why, I would have replied, "Because the Palestinians are like this and they will never relent until they get that, and the Israelis are like that and won't give in until…"

Then, quite by chance, I happened to read an Israeli novel, David Grossman's *See Under: Love.* It was exceptionally good, so I read another Israeli novel and then yet another. They were all about Jews and I simply had to admit that I'd never known any Jews. I then started to explore Palestinian literature, came across Izzat Ghazzawi, and from there ventured on to the poetic and daring Darwish and the riotous Habibi and others... All these works were about Palestinians and reminded me that I had never known any Palestinians either—until now. In my enthusiasm, I set to work, systematically reading Israeli and Palestinian authors in various Western translations, making copious notes.

Literature is fiction and not reality—that is obvious. But literature is always about people and therefore also about reality in one way or another. It is my belief that literature can take you through the backdoor to something important, something that the media would have serious difficulties discovering.

To the extent that this is a book about the conflict in the Middle East, it is an attempt to find another way in, a cultural backdoor that might provide new perspectives. Obviously, I am not denying the tanks or suicide bombers—how could I? I just feel that they no longer tell me anything new. I want to get away from the headlines, away from Arafat[2] and Sharon and their successors—and to delve deeper into something more fundamental.

I want to reach the individual. I want to hear what people think about the "enemy" and themselves. This focus has given me a new understanding. Or more accurately, it has exploded the incredibly rigid framework we adhere to in Norway when talking about the Middle East, a framework that says that if you are an intellectual and/or left-wing, you support the Palestinians, full stop. And if you say anything positive about Israel, you're instantly placed somewhere between the Christian Democrats and the Progressive Party. Fortunately, reality is far more complex. Traveling to Israel has made me realize that there is no ISRAEL, in capital letters. Just as there is no PALESTINE.

The essential, underlying theme in this ongoing voyage of discovery is precisely what Darwish underlines, the importance of getting to know the other side. After two visits to the region, I can say with some authority that very few Jews know a Palestinian and vice versa. I have also witnessed a wall several yards high springing up between them. So I turn to literature and in earnest pose my key question: can literature play a role in helping one side to see the other? A possible starting point could be the experience of the South African writer André Brink. At the "War and Peace" conference in Tromsø, Norway, in 2001, he said that in South Africa, literature and writers were a crucial force in the efforts to dismantle the old apartheid system. Black and white authors started to read each other's books—they discovered the other side through literature—and then they started to meet in person. Brink asked, what is literature? Literature is being drawn into the experience of the other. He concluded that it is imperative to understand the "enemy's" literature.

Without drawing any parallels between Israel and South Africa, is it possible to imagine a similar shift in relations between Israeli Jews and Palestinians? A couple of basic premises have to be in place before it is at all possible. First and foremost, they have to have *access* to each other's literature. This means that Palestinian literature must be translated into Hebrew and published in Israel, and Hebrew literature must be translated into Arabic and be published in Palestine. And the Israelis and Palestinians have to be both interested and willing to read each other's literature. Does this interest exist? If not, how can it be generated? Do Israeli children read Palestinian/Arabic literature at school? Do they learn Arabic? And what about the authors themselves, do they read the literature of their colleagues on the other side of the divide?

Meeting the "other" in the other side's literature is one issue. At this point, however, I would like to add the ideas of the deceased Palestinian author Izzat Ghazzawi to Brink's. At the conference in Tromsø mentioned above, Ghazzawi said that the problem with discussing literature's potential role in the conflict in the Middle East is that there are no myths of harmony and fraternization between the Jews and the Palestinians. And in the wake of this hypothesis I have my own questions: how does each side portray the other in its literature? When Israeli Jews write about Palestinians, what sort of images do they use? And what about when Palestinians write about Jews?

At the same time, we must never forget the starting point and the fact that we are talking about an age-old conflict. One cause is the establishment of the state of Israel in 1948, which entailed the displacement of approximately 750,000 Palestinians. Another is the Israeli occupation of the West Bank and the Gaza Strip in 1967. And yet another is the rising number of suicide-bomb attacks in Israel, spreading fear and panic. There are 420 Israeli military checkpoints scattered across the West Bank, where the residents suffer immense poverty and daily humiliation. In conflicts and wars, images of the enemy are painted on walls and they are by nature one-dimensional.

In the midst of all this, I look to literature and the writers. Are writers capable of bringing nuances to this image? Should this even be their task?

This project stems primarily from my own need to see past the exclamation marks in the newspapers, to the individual. I ask in earnest: What is a Jew, to a Jew? Why does Amos Oz call himself an Israeli Jew, in that order, whereas a younger author like Etgar Keret calls himself quite the opposite, a Jew living in Diaspora— or exile—in Israel? Isn't Israel Jewish? And what about literature, how are these questions of identity tackled in literature? Could one even say that literature helps form a sense of national identity?

And when we talk about Jewish/Israeli life and identity, what role does the Holocaust play? Israel was founded only a few years after World War II, and the Holocaust clearly had a huge impact on both the establishment and development of the country. Is the Holocaust now primarily a means by which Israel forces through its own agenda? What is the position of the Holocaust today, in Israeli literature and in day-to-day reality?

Concepts of identity are far from unambiguous, on both the Israeli and the Palestinian side. When I meet Palestinian authors, I ask: Who are you, as a Palestinian? What significance does the pan-Arabic cultural heritage have for a contemporary Palestinian writer? And who is the Palestinian in Palestinian literature—an eternal victim of Israeli aggression, or are there other images?

There is no denying that the pan-Arabic culture, literature included, is somewhat removed and alien to most people in the West. But is modern Arabic literature really so alien, once you make the effort to open a book? It also has to be said that Palestinian literature, in particular, is often seen to be rather boring, in that it is political, polemic, and full of pathos. I myself have heard numerous comments of this nature, but I did not have to look far to find something different and more appealing. Modernism is hardly an unknown concept in Arabic.

It is also important to try to pinpoint the actual position of the author and literature in Israel and Palestine. This is not the same as discussing literature's role in, for example, Norway and Sweden where conditions—economic and otherwise—are very similar. Let me make one thing clear, there is absolutely no symmetry between Israel and Palestine. Israel is in many ways like a modern Western European country. Palestine is not even an independent country, but an occupied territory—and only partly self-governed—where there is immense poverty and very little cultural infrastructure. There are several major publishing houses in Israel, just as in any other Western country, but in Palestine you would be hard pressed to find one.

An equally important, but perhaps more sensitive, issue is what the authors, for various reasons, *can* and cannot actually write about. Are they free?

My approach to these and similar questions is twofold. The main focus is on the author: I visited Israel and Palestine twice, in spring 2002 and autumn 2003, and interviewed some twenty authors. Unfortunately there was not enough room to include them all here.

The other element is the texts themselves: what actually happens in the texts that these authors have written?

The book is divided into two parts; the first concentrates on Hebrew literature and the second deals with Palestinian literature. But the *other* side (the Palestinian/the Jew) is present in both parts.

There is no security wall in this book.

And for those who are interested in knowing what the authors I interviewed thought about more pressing current issues, I would say that the vast majority of them are secular and position themselves politically somewhere to the left of center, some of them in the center. All the Israeli writers that I spoke to were against the Israeli occupation and in favor of an independent Palestinian state alongside Israel. All the Palestinian writers I met were against the occupation and for either a binational state or a Palestinian state coexisting with Israel.

Beyond this broad generalization, there are myriad greater and lesser differences and attitudes within each group that do not necessarily adhere to a clear Israeli/Palestinian divide. I discuss a number of these differences in this book, but others I have chosen not to include. Writing is also a matter of exclusion.

Very early on in my preliminary research, I realized that a considerable number of constraints would be needed to prevent the book's framework from exploding. So, it is about *living* writers. It is also about Jewish authors living and writing in Israel and about Palestinian writers living and writing in Palestine. I wanted it to be rooted in the Middle East, in other words; I wanted authors who had experienced the conflict firsthand. I have also chosen authors who have been translated into one or several Western languages.

This book has by no means been written in a vacuum: I have had help from many, many people. I would like to thank the Norwegian Nonfiction Writers' and Translators' Association and the Norwegian Critics' Association for their financial support. I would also like to thank Cappelen's committed and enthusiastic editors and the publisher, Anders Heger, who encouraged me to write the book. My thanks to Walid al-Kubaisi, who helped me with my initial contacts in Palestine and similarly, the ITHL (Institute for the Translation of Hebrew Literature), which assisted me with my Israeli contacts. A big thank you to *Klassekampen, Morgenbladet* and *Syn & Segn,* which all published interviews and articles that I wrote in Israel and Palestine. But first and foremost, I would like to thank all the authors, Israeli and Palestinian, who gave me so much of their time and experience. A special thanks goes to my "fixer" in Palestine, Izzat Ghazzawi, who unfortunately died in spring 2003, and to Mahmoud Shuqair, who was my middleman after Ghazzawi died.

—Runo Isaksen

Note on the Translation

The original interviews with the authors were conducted in English, and then cut, compiled, and translated into Norwegian for the Norwegian edition. This English-language edition was created by translating the Norwegian book and consulting with the original (English) interviews where necessary. Any quotations from works of literature are from published English translations when available, which are included in the bibliography.

—Kari Dickson

NOTES

1 Quote from BBC News Online 7 March 2000. This is not the first Darwish poem to generate controversy in Israel. In December 1987, the poem "Passing Words" was published in an Arabic weekly paper in Paris, not long after the outbreak of the first intifada. In the course of spring 1988, the poem was translated into Hebrew and printed in several Israeli papers and debated fervently in the Israeli media and the Knesset, where then Prime Minister Shamir condemned both Darwish and the poem. For more information, see Boullata (1997) and Alcalay (1988).

2 Arafat died on 11 November 2004 at the age of 75. He died at Percy Military Hospital outside Paris, and was buried the following day in his bombed headquarters in Ramallah. See also notes in chapter 10, note 2, and chapter 12, note 1.

1

What really matters is the quality of what's in our heads

Etgar Keret

The thing is, Israel has turned its back on so much Jewish heritage that in a sense, it is based on nothing. Modern Hebrew is a completely new language, we no longer speak Yiddish or Arabic. In many ways we have a brand-new culture. So what does Israel mean to me? It's a kind of limbo-sandwich, a sandwich with nothing in it.

Etgar Keret is the most popular author among young Israelis today and is therefore in a class of his own. His collections of short fiction are bestsellers in his home country and have been translated into several languages, including Arabic. He is known for his slightly absurd take on Israel and the world; his writing style is distinctive, straightforward, and bold.

We met for the first time in April 2002. In the six months previous to this, I had read volumes of Israeli and Palestinian literature while waiting for the right time to travel to the region. The situation was tense: one day everything looked black, the next it was *a little* lighter. Meetings had been set up with several authors. Things started to calm down again in March, so off I went—and ended up in the middle of chaos. Two hours before my plane landed, a suicide bomber blew himself up at a hotel in Netanya in Israel, killing some twenty civilians. Not long after, the Israeli army launched a massive offensive in the West Bank. A curfew was imposed. Arafat was kept under house arrest in Ramallah, surrounded by Israeli tanks; people were being killed left, right, and center in the West Bank, especially in the Jenin refugee camp, and there was a sharp increase in suicide bombs in Israel.[1]

Such was the backdrop of my first meeting with Etgar Keret. We met in a modern café in Tel Aviv, which was protected against possible car bombs by sandbags and an armed security guard, who brusquely demanded to check my bag for explosives. I had already interviewed five Israeli authors, aged between 30 and 72, before this meeting, and when asked, every one of them had said that Keret was the most exciting young writer in Israel.

I met Keret again in the early autumn, at the Kapittel Festival of Literature and Freedom of Speech in Stavanger, Norway. Some Palestinian writers also met him here, including Izzat Ghazzawi, who was so impressed that he immediately set about getting Keret translated into Arabic and published by Oragit, a Palestinian publishing house financed by the Norwegian Agency for Development Cooperation (NORAD). So, by the time I returned to Tel Aviv for my second visit in October 2003, Keret's short stories had already been published in Ramallah.

When we met, we talked very little about the political situation. I was more interested in hearing Keret's thoughts on fundamental questions such as Jewish identity. And what of Israeli identity? I got the impression that this was a relief for Keret, who smiled and confessed that he was not always very impressed with the focus of Western journalists.

Referring to his opening comment, I asked Keret what Israel had actually turned its back on and what being Jewish meant to him.

He began: "I feel connected to what I regard as Jewish heritage. We have a unique history. But what strikes me most is the fact that the Jews have always been cosmopolitans. I think that anti-Semitism is a direct response to the fact that Jews have always thought on two levels: 'I am French,' on the one hand, then when things start to go wrong in France, 'Well, I'm also Jewish. I think I'll pack up my bags and leave,' on the other. That is why nationalists have always hated the Jews. One characteristic of nationalism is that people only think on one level. Other elements of the Jewish heritage are a highly developed critical faculty and the ability to see yourself from outside. For example, the great

Christian heroes are those who are subservient to God, whereas Jewish heroes are those who argue with God, like Job. Look at the Talmud.[2] It's two guys having a discussion. Always be critical, never take anything for granted, that is the Jewish mindset. So when I look around and see all this Israeli nationalism, I don't feel like I'm in a Jewish country anymore. I feel that I am more Jewish than Israel is. Israel is in many ways anti-Jewish. Jewishness and nationalism do not go together. If you listen closely, you'll hear lots of anti-Jewish voices here in Israel. For example, I believe that the cause of Shimon Peres's strife is the fact that he is so Jewish. He reads books, speaks foreign languages, and likes to travel. Now, compare that with Sharon or the late Rabin: they don't read books, they only speak a couple of languages and firmly believe that Israel is the best place in the world. They were both generals and knew how to cultivate the land. There has always been an Israeli–Jewish conflict, and I personally feel more Jewish than Israel because Israel is a fucked-up nationalist country, just like all other nationalist countries. In that sense, there's no difference between Israel, France, and the UK. I see myself as a Jew living in Diaspora, or in exile in Israel. And I manage to maintain an outsider's perspective."

"What do you actually mean? Is Israeli nationalism just another way of saying Zionism?"

"No, they're not synonymous. A lot of people who would call themselves good Israelis have a very simple patriotic stance and can therefore be compared with nationalists in other countries, but that does not necessarily mean that they actively embrace Zionist ideals. The Zionist ethos is socialist, and many patriots in Israel today are capitalists, but they still see themselves as true Israelis, even though they can't be counted as true Zionists. So the Israeli national identity and the Zionist identity are not necessarily the same. Israeli national identity today is rooted in Zionism, but has developed into something more simplistic."

I mention to Keret that when I met Amos Oz [see chapter 4], he described himself as an Israeli Jew. In that order, first Israeli and then Jew. And I ask him what his thoughts are on that.

"I have always put my Jewishness first. If I had lived anywhere other than Israel, the one thing that no one could take away from me is my Jewish identity. It's something very fundamental. Imagine that there are two shops, one Jewish and one Israeli. I feel that the Jewish shop has far more to offer, because it has been there for much longer. The Israeli identity, on the other hand, has no real roots and only a very shallow sense of belonging. In other countries, you can dig out old traditions that are over 400 years old, if you want. Things are different here. In theory, an Iraqi Jew and I should have something in common, but as we haven't managed to establish what that is, we have decided to have nothing instead. There are Russians who want to sing Pushkin, I want to sing songs by a Polish poet, a Sephardic Jew[3] might want to sing something in Arabic, so we have simply agreed not to sing at all. If there is such a thing as a Jewish meeting point, then it's neither philosophical nor cultural, but pragmatic. The whole thing boils down to the question of survival."

"And with Zionism, perhaps a question of ideology?"

"Before, yes, but not anymore. You have perhaps come across the concept post-Zionist[4], which was first formulated in the early 1990s. To be fair, it has strong political connotations, but I see myself as a post-Zionist in the sense that ideology no longer plays an important role in my life, or for anyone else in my generation."

Living without a Past—and without the Holocaust

Keret talks without stopping for breath. At first glance he looks like an archetypal artist: unshaven, with messy hair and a very laid-back attitude. But when you look closer, he is obviously in remarkably good health and very alert; he doesn't smoke, doesn't eat meat, and orders a cup of tea when the waiter finally appears. I opt for coffee, light up a cigarillo and am immediately told off by an angry lady a couple of tables away. The smoke is apparently blowing straight at her, so I am forced to put it out. Keret shrugs and smiles: "Welcome to Israel!"

I continue: "You were saying that in the process of establishing Israel, Jews have lost something important."

"You can look at what Herzl, the father of Zionism, writes about the building of the nation, that it's a kind of healing process. And it's true, that was what really motivated people to come here. But the need to create something new also means that you didn't like what was there before. Having said that, I personally think that the Jewish identity and culture is one of the most incredible things to have happened in modern times. Yet we turn our back on some things. For example, something that is very symbolic for me: the year I started high school, Shalom Aleichem[5] was taken out of the curriculum. What country would decide to do that? Imagine Irish schools not teaching James Joyce—impossible. But here, and it isn't even a conspiracy, the question of identity seems to be completely irrelevant. When I asked my teacher why, he replied: 'Well, students don't understand Shalom Aleichem any more.' Philip Roth is represented by my publishers here in Israel, and my editor told me that this country has possibly the lowest sales of Roth in the world. Bernard Malamud[6] and other great Jewish writers sell more books abroad than in Israel, even though they're writing about Jewish identity. I think that it's shameful that such truly deep philosophical, moral, and cultural thinkers are just rejected—because they leave an unfortunate aftertaste of weakness. The Jewish identity is more or less despised here in Israel, not openly, not vocally, but subconsciously. You know, the Diaspora Jew, the weak one. Here in Tel Aviv you will find more sushi restaurants than Jewish restaurants, as if Jewish food is not good enough. I think that this denial of Jewish identity is often due to a lack of self-irony, which may in fact have helped us to accept weakness. The new Jew, the Israeli Jew, has to be strong and proud."

"And that will make Israel a strong and proud nation?"

'The Diaspora Jews, especially those in Europe, always saw themselves as a minority, living at the mercy of a great power, whether that was the czar, the king, or anyone else. The creation of the state of Israel turned this image upside down: we say we are the strong ones now, responsible for our own decisions and actions. But at the same time we suffer from a kind of inferiority complex. As a nation, we nurture the idea that we are strong, but deep down, we feel weak and persecuted, sometimes even paranoid in relation to anyone who criticizes us. Our history is so full of pogroms and persecution that we live in constant fear of being wiped out, that Jews as such will cease to exist. Will I exist in the future? This question is also relevant with regard to Israel."

When I ask whether it is possible in Hebrew literature to differentiate between authors who are more Jewish and others who are more Israeli, Keret replies: "There are a lot of very good Israeli authors, but humor is not a driving force in their writing. For example, when you read Oz, Grossman, or A.B. Yehoshua[7] you are not immediately struck by the fact that they are funny or self-critical in an ironic way, in the same way as Diaspora Jews, such as Woody Allen or Isaac Singer.[8] Even though most contemporary Israeli writers have Jewish roots, in that they have a knowledge of Jewish history, they don't normally demonstrate a Jewish mentality. As a reader, I feel much closer to Martin Buber[9] than A.B. Yehoshua. Jewish literature has always been more concerned with humanist ideas than nationalist ones, and has always been more interested in the subtext than the text itself."

Jewish identity versus Israeli identity is a motif in many of Keret's short stories. "The Son of the Head of Mossad" is about precisely that. The father is the head of the Israeli intelligence service, Mossad, and the son is portrayed as a negative image of him: skinny and not very heroic. Palestinian writer Mahmoud Shuqair mentioned this short story in particular when I met him in October 2003. He chuckled and commented on the sense of humor that is always bubbling just under the surface, and how liberating Keret's position is. "Keret doesn't preach ideology," Shuqair explained, "only humanity."

Keret nods and sips his by now cold tea. "It is about a young Israeli's identity. We're expected to follow in our ancestors' footsteps. But look at Zionism: the ideals were completely abstract, and we were never allowed to even question them. The most famous children's book in Israel has an invisible hero, twelve-year-old Danny Dean, who works for the secret service. No coincidence that the greatest hero of children's literature is invisible. He is a role model that you cannot see and can barely imagine. So you could say that my short story is about Danny Dean's son. There is a generation gap. The father lives in a very simple right-and-wrong world. So he is a fairly classical Israeli, à la Sharon or Rabin or Moshe Dayan, who has never had any kind of inner struggle and always does the right thing. His son, on the other hand, is typically Jewish, and he also has a typical Diaspora name, not a Hebrew one. In other words, the older generation steered a steady course, whereas the younger generation are the doubting, self-reflecting Jews who don't know the answers."

Keret claims that in the process of establishing the state of Israel in 1948, Zionism declared: "No one brings anything from the past with them."

"Except the Holocaust," I protest. "Because the Holocaust has almost become an alternative Jewish religion, has it not?"

"Well, the Holocaust has always been something to be kept at arm's length. This country does not like Holocaust survivors. They want the Holocaust to be a symbol of their rebirth. But I believe that when you're reborn, you should also confront your old identity. Just look at what happens when young Israelis go to Auschwitz— they plant the Israeli flag there! The Israeli flag—even though no Israelis were killed there, due to the simple fact that Israel did not yet exist. I also find it astonishing that young people here show absolutely no interest in knowing how the Jews lived in Poland. They only want to know how they died. If you ask people on the street, they wouldn't be able to tell you the name of a single Polish Jewish poet or writer, but they could, without any hesitation, tell you exactly how many Jews died in any of the Polish concentration camps. Jewishness is just a platform for creating an Israeli identity. The Holocaust is important. After all, it's the reason why we had to become strong and adopt new values. Because the old ones, being philosophical, self-critical, and cosmopolitan, were no longer valid."

"But is it really possible to reject the past and live without it?"

"I truly believe that we live in a country where no one knows anything about their own past. Look at me, for example. My parents are Polish, but I can't speak Polish and I know nothing about Polish literature. Some of our conservative politicians grumble that most people don't even know the words of our national anthem. I'm not saying that it's *important* to know the words, I'm just pointing out that we live in a country where most people don't know the national anthem, in fact where most people, even if they were born here, can't even speak Hebrew properly."

"Really?"

"People are constantly making bigger or smaller mistakes. I do too. Because our shared foundation is so hollow and unrooted, and because we're so fixated on the future and indifferent to the past, we don't even offer students any real grounding, we just say: 'Study technology.' There seems to be no need for recognizing—or respecting—anything that might form a kind of corpus. So yes, we do struggle with an identity that is arbitrary and split. Zionism is riddled with paradoxes; it's like starting up a computer program only to discover that it contains a virus. Over the years, the virus contaminates more and more, and in the end you just have to accept that your PC no longer works. I think that my generation has realized this and we now clearly recognize the problems and can face them squarely. We lack the tools to resolve them, but recognizing them is a step forward, compared with the last generation. And who knows, maybe the next generation will even know how to solve them."

Translation and Teaching

Moving on from Israel's internal struggles, I ask about its Arab neighbors, and the Palestinians in particular, and whether literature can play a role in the conflict with Palestine.

The question assumes that literature can in fact influence people and achieve great things, which immediately gives rise to another: is that perhaps a somewhat overoptimistic assessment of literature? I take with me to the table André Brink's experience from South Africa.

I explain to Etgar Keret, who has himself been translated into Arabic and published in Ramallah, that in South Africa the point was not so much that the blacks and the whites suddenly loved one another, but that they started to discover each other through literature, to see the other side as human beings.

He replies: "I was speaking to the Palestinian poet Ghassan Zaqtan [see chapter 9], who is a good friend of mine, and he told me that my book had sold out in Ramallah. I commented that people were probably just curious about Israeli literature. He replied, 'No, they buy your books because your work is different from other Israeli authors and it's what they want to see.' As an Israeli author, I'm more interested in Palestinian literature that is *not* directly about the conflict. Similarly, Palestinians don't want to read Israeli books that tell them who they are, but rather ones that might tell them who *I* am—that is what is interesting. Apropos of South Africa, Nadine Gordimer always tries to deal with the conflict and find solutions, and I tend to find her books rather uninteresting. But it's quite the opposite with J.M. Coetzee. He really captures the complexity of the situation and that is a valuable contribution. I don't need someone to show me what's right and wrong, I *know* what is wrong. Instead I need someone who says, 'This is reality.' So what I would look for in the Israeli–Palestinian dialogue is something that is normally denied, something that people think, but don't say. Because what we hear today is nothing more than a bunch of clichés. If you gathered together the work of all Israeli and Palestinian writers over the past 30 years, and fed their texts into a PC, you would see that 90 percent of the words they use are identical. I do it too. Every time I'm asked to write an article or an essay, the first thing I do is sit down in front of my computer and write a paragraph, before reading it through and discovering all the familiar words: 'tragedy,' 'unbearable,' etc. So many words that are supposed to describe the situation, but in fact what they do is build a wall between you and reality. Because the truth is—even now, during the second intifada—life here is not unbearable. It is tragic, but life elsewhere is tragic as well. There is no inherent difference between my fear of being blown to bits by a suicide bomber and your fear of developing cancer or getting fired. We're both human and we're both frightened of dying. But here the situation binds us together with a sort of chain of clichés."

Keret leans back in his chair and frowns: "I'm talking an awful lot today. Just stop me if you have any questions."

I assure him that nothing makes an interviewer more happy than an interviewee who talks, and what is more, the MiniDisc that I have with me will ensure that every word is recorded. I don't need to do anything other than listen and decide what to ask next. For example:

"If you read work by the Palestinian poet Mahmoud Darwish [see chapter 14], who I know has been translated into Hebrew, is it possible to get an idea of the Palestinian psyche?"

"Yes, of course, I can gain a better understanding of Palestinians through their literature. But at the same time, I think that it is fairly usual to overestimate the effect that literature has on people. It's best to meet people face to face."

"What about translation from Arabic into Hebrew, in general? If I go into any of the Israeli-owned Steimatzky bookstores, will I find Palestinian authors there?"

"No. There is a clear lack of knowledge about Israel on the Palestinian side, but likewise there is a clear lack of knowledge here in Israel about Palestine and Palestinian literature. A handful of Palestinian authors have been translated into Hebrew, but not enough by a long shot. Darwish has, but all in all, very little has been translated. Looking at Palestinians living here in Israel, there are not many writers among them. But if those who do live here were to write in Hebrew, they would have a greater chance, like Anton Shammas with *Arabesques* and Sayed Kashua, who recently had a bestseller with *Dancing Arabs*.[10] Salman Natour [see chapter 15] plays a role as an intellectual. But few have managed to get past that barrier and reach out to a wider Israeli readership."

"What about schools, do pupils study Palestinian literature in Israeli schools?"

"Well, in the course of my twelve years of obligatory schooling,

I was only introduced to one Arabic writer, and that was the Egyptian Nobel Prize winner Naguib Mahfouz. One single Arabic book—and I live in the Middle East! I must have read around twenty times more Russian and French literature than I have Arabic, which is a terrible state of affairs."

"Do you think there are political reasons for that?"

"Well, it's more that Israel likes to see itself as a European country. We take part in the Eurovision Song Contest, we are always losing in the UEFA Cup. Look around, we're sitting in a European café, aren't we? The people on the street think they can jump on a local bus, pull the cord and get off in Paris. In my day, French was a far more popular third language than Arabic—but why do you need French here? Who can you talk to? Everyone around you speaks Arabic. It's completely crazy. When I was in Ohio recently, I was asked to give a good metaphor for Israel. And I said that Israel is like a casino in Las Vegas. You come in from the desert, someone opens the door and says: 'Welcome to Rome!' Then you wander around among the palaces, go up in the elevator and get to Venice, where a gondola takes you to your room. That's what it is like here, it's Europe. We haven't accepted the fact that we're in the fucking Middle East. But on the other hand when I look around, what do I see? Egypt, where you can be sent to jail for kissing a man on the street; Syria, where people are shot in the head at demonstrations; and then there's Jordan, and Iraq. So, what can I say? I live in Israel, which is geographically positioned in the Middle East, and I go to concerts and listen to Mahler. It's a fundamental problem, but that is what makes Israel exciting. We are a living paradox."

There has been at least one change since Keret left school: Mahmoud Darwish has been introduced into the high-school curriculum. And in Keret's view, education, in particular, is extremely important.

"The main problem with the Oslo Accords was that everyone was interested in the political perspective, but no one was interested in the social one. If I was forced to create peace, I would say: 'I want international observers here, not to check if the

Palestinians have weapons—they can have all the weapons they like—but rather to monitor their schools.' I would ensure that every Palestinian classroom had a map that actually shows Israel, and I would make them read about us in their textbooks. Because accords and agreements are always about territories, but territories are nothing—what really matters is the quality of what's in our heads.'

The Writer as Prophet

Can a writer achieve something completely unique simply by virtue of being a writer? Even in a peaceful country like Norway, people called for writers to protest when the US bombed Iraq. I turn to the writer's position in Israel. What, in Etgar Keret's opinion, is the role of Hebrew literature and writers in Israel? And what is the relationship like between older, acclaimed writers and younger writers?

As I mull over these questions, formulating them in my mind, Keret suddenly asks what my impression of Israel is so far. How do I answer a question like that? I tell him about episodes at bus stops where people have as good as vanished as soon as I opened my bag to take out a bottle of water. They think that I'm about to detonate a bomb. I admit that I feel as if I'm being watched. I feel guilty, even though I, of course, have done nothing and have no plans to do anything—and I put on a bizarre act to convince the world that I'm innocent. With my third eye, I observe both myself, and this ridiculous act I have chosen to perform.

Keret then asks how I was received here, what my first meeting with Israel was like. This is a question I am asked time and again, by both Jews and Palestinians. How long did it take you to get through customs? What did they ask? Did you have to get undressed?

The funny thing is that I can now tell a true story about the power of literature. It goes like this: I flew from Bergen to Tel Aviv, with a transfer at Schipol in Amsterdam. This was where I was to go through the main security check, so I was asked to be at the gate at least two hours before departure. The line was long and tedious, but finally it was my turn. After a series of preliminary questions about my suitcase—who owned it, who had packed it, etc.—we got to the purpose of my visit. I told them openly and enthusiastically about my book and the response was a volley of questions: can you prove that you are a writer? Can you prove that you have meetings set up in Israel? Why do you have an Egyptian visa in your passport? And Syrian? What were you doing in Syria? What were you doing in Lebanon? After a long time, the interrogator withdrew to confer with a mysterious woman who was half hidden by a partition wall. Proof, I thought to myself, how can I prove that what I'm saying is true? Then I remembered my address book, with the names and telephone numbers of Amos Oz and David Grossman and the whole lot. So when the interrogator returned with a furrowed brow, I handed him my address book and said, "Here is the list of authors I'm going to meet, both Israeli and Palestinian. You can just call them if you want to confirm it." He took the address book over to the Israeli policewoman. Not long after, he came back smiling and said, "Do you know what the Israeli policewoman said? 'But they're famous! Can I get a copy of these pages?' Thank you for being so patient and understanding, sir. Have a good journey."

Could it be that this little story reveals something about the position of authors and literature in Israel today? Keret nods.

"Biblical prophet, that is the role traditionally assigned to the writer in this country. We recognize him from television interviews, sitting there in his suit, with his pipe and politically correct left-wing ideas. Filmed with a low-angle camera, and the Tower of David in the background, he says things like, 'I believe that the only solution to the conflict in the Middle East is…' My generation has grown up with these images and we know that it's bullshit. I also think that their dour seriousness has put lots of potential readers off literature, whereas some of the truly great authors, such as Nabokov, Faulkner, Dostoevsky, and Bulgakov are actually very funny. Here in Israel, it is absolutely not the done thing to say I write books that are funny. We suffer from the Thomas Mann syndrome—if a book is 700 pages long and difficult to read, then it must be really deep! Sometimes it is, true enough, but I think there are other ways of being deep."

Many of Keret's readers are the sort of people who generally do not read books. A survey carried out by the bookstore chain Steinmatzky has shown that Keret's books are at the top of the most-stolen books list. He believes that he has become so popular because he writes about the reality of today's young people.

"In Israel, as an author, you're expected to generate both fiction and political opinion—even though you don't necessarily have a talent for both."

"Younger writers like yourself are politically less vocal than say, Grossman or Oz?"

"Well, a lot of young writers participate in the political debate. But the fact that young writers don't assume the traditional role is a kind of protest, yes."

"Do you find Amos Oz's commitment pathetic?"

"No, just different. He is traditional and inhabits a sphere where the writer is smarter than the reader. And that is a fundamentally different position from my own."

"And where is the literary divide between generations?"

"Traditional literature places ideology in the foreground and human beings in the background. It's the other way around with me, I put people in front. When you wake up in the morning in Israel, your first thought, according to traditional literature, is: 'What is the future of the Middle East?' *My* first thought is: 'Why doesn't my girlfriend love me any more?' or 'I hope no one has stolen my car.' Then I get up and have a cup of coffee and then— but not before—I may have my first political thought. And I try to reflect this in my writing. I'm often criticized because my texts don't have an ideological bottom line, but I think that literature can still be moral, even if it doesn't have a bottom line. That would be like shouting at Kafka in the Prague of his day: 'You hedonistic pig, you may write well about metamorphosis, but why don't you write about unemployment or the persecution of the gypsies?' You can be moral in different ways. An SS officer in a concentration camp would still find it very difficult to continue doing his job after reading Kafka, even though Kafka doesn't write about Nazis. So I want to get away from ideological texts and to dig deeper into the subtext. The point is that we've become blind and deaf to the subtext, we only live at the text level. My short story 'The Bus Driver Who Wanted to be God,' is about that. The bus driver's ideology justifies his failure to stop and let the late arriver on the bus. You might say that it is about how ideology can prevent us from seeing the person in front of us, because he or she has been reduced to a label. And that's a very Israeli thing to do, because Israel is such a fragmented society. It's also about how you may be ideologically right, but still behave inhumanely. Life is not really about being right or wrong, so much as dealing with other people. The driver suddenly sees the man outside as another human being, so he stops the bus and opens the door, even though it's wrong from an ideological point of view. And that doesn't happen very often here in the Middle East. It's a rare thing that the doors open and someone thinks, 'He's different from me, but he's just someone who wants to get somewhere on time.' So I say, to hell with right and wrong."

Keret thinks he has also discovered another literary difference between generations. "Traditionally, the left-wing in Israel has told the story of our great collective history. A typical constellation of characters in an Israeli film from the '80s would be an officer, an Israeli Arab, a religious figure, and a Holocaust survivor. Israel in micro format. Personally, I don't want that responsibility, instead I say, 'I'm going to tell you what *I* saw.' You see, my generation is trying to turn this pyramid on its head and to tell the story of the outsider, so that he is the focus, not the collective. The best films in recent years have been those that tell the story of one person, not of society or a community. This is revolutionary. Many of my own stories have been filmed. It is now accepted in Israeli cinema that Israel is a multicultural society. The Zionists could not accept that, and preferred to talk about a melting pot. But they forgot that people don't melt, they burn. Before, the stories of the officer and the Holocaust survivor were supposed to intertwine to weave a kind of togetherness. Nowadays, people say: 'Dorit Rabinyan [see chapter 7] has her story, and Etgar Keret has his and that's okay.' I don't need to have an Iranian in my books, and equally Dorit doesn't need to have an unemployed, fucked-up guy in his twenties in hers."

Even though politically Keret is left-wing, he does not feel an inherent affinity with left-wing radicals. "Lefties are not like me. They're arrogant and unsophisticated. The fact that we share the same ideology is of less importance. I would rather have an ultra-Orthodox Jew with a warm heart as a friend than a distorted left-wing bastard, but in Israel, you're not allowed to say things like that. A typical first question on a blind date would be, 'What party do you vote for?' But I have said goodbye to ideology, I don't want to hear your manifesto. I would rather ask: who are you, as a person?"

Keret pauses, just long enough for me to ponder the answer: who am *I*, as a person? Then he nods and concludes, "So, the main issue here in Israel is whether you see the other person, or not, whether you can relate to him. That is far more important than your political leaning."

"But, in terms of politics, what do you think your role as a writer is?"

"What makes me a good writer, if in fact I am a good writer, is that I acknowledge my own weaknesses. I have so many weaknesses that I have a constant source of material for new stories. My role is to point out what is wrong, not to say how we can get out of this mess. I say: this is fucked up—and that's good enough for me. I'm not Oz or Grossman, I have no new plans for the Middle East. Some critics like to scream that writers have a moral responsibility. Well, I'm responsible for my own morals, not anyone else's."

"Let me ask you the great, overriding, and no doubt difficult question: what are you trying to achieve as a writer?"

Keret laughs.

"I was starting to get a bit worried there, but that's easy. For me, literature's greatest power is the potential to unbalance you. Normally we go around on auto-pilot. I want to give you a push, so that you are forced to reorient yourself: what is up and what is down? It's like cycling: I can ride a bike, but I don't have a good explanation as to why I don't fall. Literature forces you to ask the question: how can I cycle and not fall? That is what I look for in literature, not descriptions of pain, or flowery language, and all the colors of the rainbow. No, I look for a human undercurrent that suddenly erupts in your face."

Seeing the Other—through a Peephole

Few Israeli Jews can put their hand on their heart and say that they know, really know, a Palestinian. And it is also true that very little Arabic—and even less Palestinian—literature is translated into Hebrew and published in Israel. Given the situation, I wonder where Jews should look in order to understand Palestinians. I ask Keret about modern Hebrew literature and how the Palestinian is portrayed there.

"An American producer once threw money at me and shouted: 'Make a film about a Palestinian suicide bomber and a Jew—two parallel stories.' And I replied: 'To be honest, I can't write about a fundamentalist Muslim with any respect. I have no idea what goes on inside his head. To me, he's just mad.' I've been translated into Arabic and the response to precisely that, the fact that I see Palestinians as alien, has been positive; the fact that I don't use the traditional, patronizing Israeli leftist voice, à la A.B. Yehoshua. His most famous short story, 'Facing the Forest,' is about a Jew and an Arab, but the Arab is dumb, so the Jew describes what the Arab feels and wants. In that way, the author colonizes the Palestinian's identity. They claim to understand the Arab mentality and subconscious. Explaining what the other person wants is an Israeli tradition, and I'm trying to change that. Because if you say to a Palestinian, 'I understand your pain, I will explain it to you,' then you're not on an equal footing. What I say is that there are other people here as well, and they are very, very angry, but I can't tell you exactly what it is they want."

"So how do you portray Arabs/Palestinians yourself?"

"I present them from my viewpoint. I have a tiny little peephole through which I can see them, but I can only see what I encounter, so I can tell you a lot about my own fears, and very little about them. The Arab mentality is strange and alien to me. Just take the fact that they keep a note of the dates of their dead. Ask any Israeli when the Dolphinarium bomb exploded[11] and he won't have a clue. We're talking about different mentalities. Sometimes differences are quaint and exciting, and other times they scare the living daylights out of you."

Keret does not agree with the hypothesis proposed by Izzat Ghazzawi in Tromsø in September 2001. According to Ghazzawi, the problem is that there are no stories of bonding between Jews and Palestinians. Keret, on the other hand, believes that the Israeli left nurtures a romantic idea of Israeli–Palestinian friendship.

"This friendship has always been there, but only as a dream, not as a reflection of reality. The fact is that the left-wing in Israel sees Palestinians through Western eyes. So when Barak meets Arafat, it's like Bill Gates meeting an executive director who he wants to do business with. But we live in the fucking Middle East, where people have been killing each other for centuries. You have to adjust to the mentality here. Personally, I would love to see much more written about the suspicion that exists between Jews and Palestinians—stories that acknowledge these things. Imagine living in a society where homophobia prevailed. You would want to see that homophobia reflected in literature, wouldn't you? You wouldn't want to read stories about homosexuals and other people living together in perfect harmony."

Keret does not write books to demonstrate that Palestinians are also human. He writes about his own society, about Jews in Israel—and for them, Palestinians/Arabs are *the stranger*, someone you don't really know. So how does this manifest itself in his writings?

The short story "Cocked and Locked" is about an encounter between a young Israeli soldier and an unpleasant Hamas activist, and about mutual hate. This is one of several short stories by Keret that have caused controversy in Israel. The story ends with the soldier smashing the Hamas activist against a streetlight again and again. So what does that signify—that the evil Palestinian gets what he deserves?

Keret does not agree with this interpretation. He believes that the short story is not biased. "The story is not about politics, it's about the psychological processes people go through when they are part of a violent occupation. This country has ideological arguments for and against the occupation, but no one talks about what happens to young soldiers when they have been in the army for three years, three years of violence. And we wonder why people stab each other on the streets of Tel Aviv. People don't understand where it's coming from. And no one sees the gaping chasm between our ideas and real life. I have many left-wing friends who have demonstrated against the occupation one day, only to find themselves moving into the West Bank as soldiers the next, and suddenly beating people senseless. I mean, just because you're a child psychologist doesn't mean that you won't still suddenly hit your child. It's possible. I wanted to write a story that was not just an observation of the situation, but that came from my gut, from an existential viewpoint. About the soldier's envy of his Hamas opponent, because the soldier is weighed down by doubt and there's no room for that in violent confrontation. The Hamas activist, for his part, has absolute faith. He knows what he wants, and I don't know what I want, and that gives him power. For me, the conclusion of the story is that you can't occupy a moral high ground. Moral occupation is an impossibility."

Victim Theory

Despite portraying Palestinians as *the other side* in his literary universe, Keret points to a number of parallels between Jews and Palestinians.

"Since the Holocaust, we Jews have seen ourselves as absolute victims. If anyone tries to moralize, we simply say, 'Right, and where were you when the Holocaust happened?' If Norway only gives us three points in the Eurovision Song Contest, we say, 'We've heard about Quisling, we know what goes on in your country.' I did think that this attitude was in the process of dying out, but then it was revived under Sharon. The main problem with the role of victim is that no suffering is equal to your own, which means there is no scope for empathy with others. If a Palestinian says, 'They destroyed my home,' you just reply, 'You call that destruction? Come with me to Poland, and I'll show you what happened to *my* home.' We were in the process of healing and had passed the role of victim on to the Palestinians, who now use a typically Jewish rhetoric. There are great similarities between us, you know. We both have a rather fucked-up history, and we use it justify our lack of empathy with others."

"You said you thought that attitude was about to die out. What was it that revived it again?"

"The murder of Rabin in 1995. Before that, from the end of the '80s and into the '90s, there was a movement toward the secularization of the Jewish state, and we said, 'We're not the chosen people, we're just people. The anti-Semites wanted to kill us, so we came here, but now we can be a normal country.' This lost momentum when Rabin was murdered, and the separatists gained ground, that is, the people who say, 'We are radically different from other people.'"

"How is the role of victim expressed by the Palestinians?"

"Let me take a slight detour: there isn't a single Arabic textbook that deals with the Holocaust. Why? Because that would unravel the whole notion of yourself as absolute victim. I have several close Palestinian friends who are smart and intelligent people, but when I mention the Holocaust, they say, 'Yes, I've heard about that. But only 4,000 people were killed.' It's a defense mechanism. Because the minute you admit that someone else's pain is greater than your own, you're forced to empathize. You can see the same thing happening in Israel these days. When someone talks about the tragedy in Jenin, which was truly horrific, our instinctive response is: 'How can you talk about Jenin, when…'"

Keret believes that there are similarities in Palestinian and Israeli rhetoric. "A well-known Palestinian intellectual once said,

'The Middle East is a football match, and the Palestinians are always the ball.' Statements like that have very powerful and dangerous moral consequences. If you are the ball and break someone's nose, then you're not guilty, because a ball has no control. So, if you are a suicide bomber, how can anyone judge you? Of course, that's all total bullshit. My parents lived in the Warsaw ghetto during the Second World War, but they never even dreamed about massacring German children. The truth is, you will find very few Palestinians who do not see suicide bombers as *sjahid,* that is, martyrs. Even if they are against this form of struggle, they would never say, 'They're crazy.' Even *they* feel a strong empathy with suicide bombers. For me, it is a very, very Jewish syndrome: our suffering is so great that no one has the right to come here and judge our actions."

Israeli Taboos

A key question in my discussions with both Palestinian and Israeli writers has been whether they feel free. Is there anything that they can't write about or find it difficult to write about?

Most Israelis smile and shake their heads. No, no, I am free. But not Keret. For him, Israeli taboos are very much alive.

"There is a strong link between personal grief and national taboos in this country. And those taboos are soldiers who have died fighting, the Holocaust, and not least how the Holocaust and victims of terrorism are honored, including Rabin. I personally lost my best friend in the army. He didn't actually die fighting, he committed suicide. So for me, memorials for fallen soldiers are something very personal. And you know, my whole family—with the exception of my parents—died in Europe during the Holocaust, so the memory of the Holocaust is also a personal memory. There is always a tension between personal and national memories. The question is whether I can keep my personal memory when national memorials force you to comply with a fixed method. When my friend was buried, an officer gave a speech and said that my friend was very courageous, and that his fellow soldiers loved him. But the truth is that my friend was a coward and all the other soldiers hated him. You see, if you die as a soldier or the victim of a suicide bomb, or you died during the Holocaust, you're no longer allowed to be yourself. You are depersonalized. Short stories like 'Rabin's Dead,' 'Shoes,' and 'Siren' are about people trying to keep their own personal memories instead of just swallowing some pre-digested mush. Many Israelis were enraged by 'Rabin's Dead.' They thought it was disrespectful to write about a cat called Rabin that died. But if you think about it, why is it disrespectful to call a cat you love after Rabin, when calling a geriatric nursing home after him isn't? Who decides? Your grief is nationalized, it is no longer yours, it is *ours*, and we will tell you how to deal with it."

"In the story 'Shoes,' the boy finally puts on the shoes that represent the memory of his father who was killed in the Holocaust.'

"Yes, 'Shoes' illustrates the two different versions of the Holocaust that I know: the one from school and the other from my home, from my parents who lost their siblings and parents in the Warsaw ghetto. The official version is the one where six million people were killed and there is a black marble mausoleum for them, where you are not allowed to touch anything, say anything, or question anything. And the fact that you can't touch somehow distances you from it. It's not an emotional experience, but rather a fossilized one. I don't think a child is capable of understanding the figure six million. My dad always said, 'I'm a person and I have had an extreme experience. But do you really think that my feelings back then were so very different from your own feelings today? I was frightened, hungry, and angry. But you also know what it means to be frightened, hungry, and angry. It's just a matter of quantity. The Holocaust is not something extraterrestrial, it's part of life.' He didn't live in another galaxy, just somewhere that was more extreme than where I live now. So yes, the story ends with the shoes becoming part of the boy, something that is always with him, even though he forgets now and then, and the shoes get dirty—they're an integral part of his life, and not something extraterrestrial."

"I know that 'Siren' has also provoked some very strong reactions here in Israel."

"Yes, it's included in the high-school curriculum, and a lot of teachers refuse to teach it. They don't think that it is edifying: a hero who ignores the law and keeps moving when the siren for fallen soldiers sounds. They're probably frightened that the pupils will be corrupted by it. Many of them are not even aware that it is *possible* to move when the siren is howling. For me, it is yet another example of what happens when the symbol supplants the memory. To me, these national symbols are like conquerors, they vanquish your memory, eat into it, become part of it, so that in the end, it is no longer possible to separate one from the other."

"How do these taboos—what you have just defined as taboos, i.e., soldiers killed fighting, the Holocaust and victims of terrorism—work in practice?"

"You must not criticize them. And you must not humanize them. But I do, I'm always writing about them in my short stories."

"What do you think links the three things?"

"It's the tension between personal grief, on the one hand, and the way in which it's used to create a future identity for the country, on the other."

"So in a way, it's a kind of nation-building, or something that unifies the country?"

"I certainly think that all three things help to underline the need for Israel's continued existence."

"And maybe that has something to do with the role of the victim as well?"

"Something in the myth of the victim fuels the myth of heroism. You only have two choices: to be a victim or a hero. There is no third option."

"But if there was, would the alternative be to be human?"

Keret shrugs and thinks about it. He has been talking for several hours now and is starting to get bored of his own voice. We pay our bill, leave a healthy tip, and get up.

"To be human? That doesn't seem to be particularly relevant to most people around here."

He holds out his right hand, shakes mine, thanks me for my interest and patience, and apologizes for having talked far too much, before smiling, turning around and sauntering off down the pavement.

NOTES

1 For a Palestinian insight into the siege of Ramallah in 2002, see Shehadeh (2004). Shehadeh, an attorney, lives and works in Ramallah and his diary is not really about power politics, but more about day-to-day business and humiliation under the Israeli occupation.

2 The Talmud: Judaism's code of law and commentary, comprising the Mishnah (written down in the third century CE) and the rabbinical commentary on it, the Gemara (written down in the sixth century CE).

3 Sephardim, Sephardi, Sephardic Jew: originally referred to Jews from Spain, in other words, the Jews who were driven from Spain in 1492 and who then later settled along the eastern shores of the Mediterranean, and whose customs and rituals are distinct from those of Ashkenazi (or European) Jews. The term is also used more generally to describe "Oriental Jews," that is, Jews from the Middle East and North Africa, including Arab countries; the term Mizrahim (or Mizrahi Jews) is also commonly used as an umbrella term for Jews from this range of backgrounds. For more about the differences between Mizrahi and Ashkenazi Jews, see the interview with Dorit Rabinyan, chapter 7.

4 Post-Zionism evolved around the periodical *Teoriya vi-Bekorit* (*Theory and Criticism*) in the early 1990s. It is critical of Zionism, Israel's leading ideology, and builds on postcolonial theory and a critical assessment of the concept of multiculturalism. Much has been written on the subject. For a critical overview, see Matta (2003).

5 Shalom Aleichem is Yiddish for "peace be with you." This was the pseudonym of Salom Rabinovic (1859–1916), a Jewish author born in the Ukraine. He wrote in Russian and Hebrew, but primarily in Yiddish. He wrote poems, plays, stories, and novels. The musical *The Fiddler on the Roof* is based on one of his novels. His work portrays Eastern European Jews with satire and gentle humor.

6 Bernard Malamud (1914–1986). American author of Russian Jewish descent. He wrote several short-story collections and novels, including *The Natural* and *The Fixer*.

7 A.B. Yehoshua (born 1936). Recognized as one of Israel's greatest

living writers. He made his literary debut in 1962 and has since published a number of novels, short-story collections, essay collections, and plays. He has been translated into many languages. For David Grossman, see chapter 2, and for Amos Oz, see chapter 5.

8 Isaac Bashevis Singer (1904–1991), novelist and short-story writer, was born in Poland but emigrated to the US in 1935. He wrote in Yiddish throughout his life, and his books were later translated into English and other languages. Bashevis Singer was awarded the Nobel Prize for Literature in 1978.

9 Martin Buber (1878–1965) was an Austrian Jewish theologian and philosopher. He worked at the University of Frankfurt am Main (as a professor from 1930) and then from 1937 he was professor of the philosophy of religion at the University of Jerusalem. He wrote a number of books, the best known being *Ich und Du* (1923).

10 Anton Shammas (born 1950 in Fassuta, Israel) is a professor of literature and has lived and worked in Michigan for many years. His novel *Arabesques,* published in 1986, was written in Hebrew. It has been translated into eight languages, including English. He has also published two poetry collections in both Hebrew and Arabic. Sayed Kashua (born 1975) had great success with his novel, *Dancing Arabs,* published in spring 2002. The book was written in Hebrew and has been translated into many languages. His novel *Vayehi Boker* (*Let It Be Morning*) was published in 2004, in English in 2006.

11 Keret is talking about the suicide bomb attack at the Dolphinarium disco in Tel Aviv on 1 June 2001. Twenty-one people were killed and 120 injured, most of them teenagers from Russia.

2

In morality's catastrophe zones

David Grossman

My conversations with many Palestinian authors and intellectuals have given me the distinct impression that David Grossman is the most appreciated living Israeli writer among Palestinians today. Some of Grossman's books have been translated into Arabic and his articles are regularly translated. His nonfiction books go straight to the heart of the Israeli–Palestinian conflict, books in which Grossman gives space to the Palestinian viewpoint and allows the Palestinians to tell their own stories.

His books for children and young people are also highly valued in his home country and most Israelis today grow up with Grossman. In other countries, in addition to his works of nonfiction, he is best known for his novels for adults: great epic works, some of them rather experimental.

Before I went to Israel for the first time in April 2002, I talked to Grossman and made a loose arrangement to meet. I then phoned him several times from a crackly public telephone in Palestinian East Jerusalem, but he was uncertain, he wasn't sure whether it would be possible, he had so much to do, he needed to protect himself. I insisted that the book I wanted to write would never come to much if I didn't meet him in particular. I rang Izzat Ghazzawi in Ramallah when the entire town was under a round-the-clock curfew, with only Israeli tanks allowed on the streets. My whole project seemed to be doomed, but Ghazzawi would hear no such thing; he believed that it was now more important than ever to interview writers, Israeli and Palestinian, and to hold the banner of hope and peace high.

"I'll call David Grossman later. He's a good friend of mine. He will meet you." I still didn't manage to meet Grossman in spring 2002, but we did meet the next time I was in Israel.

As a journalist, Grossman might growl and snap, but the man I met at the YMCA in West Jerusalem one day in October 2003 was a calm, soft-spoken man.

"Writers here tend to write about what they see and experience, rather than science fiction. It wouldn't be natural to write about *positive* intense relationships between Israelis and Palestinians. When you read books—usually foreign—about a relationship between an Israeli soldier and a Palestinian woman, it always rings untrue because basically it would never happen in reality. And the reason for that is perhaps the way in which Israelis perceive Palestinians and the sexual attributes that they believe Palestinian women to have or not have. The problem is that you don't see the other side as real people. So there are very few or no such relationships, despite the fact that the friction between the two peoples is immense."

For Grossman, literature is about seeing the other side. A writer is someone who has the ability to see the world from many different angles at the same time, and that is what makes literature so powerful.

"Ideally, writers should study all aspects of human phenomena. What do I expect from a writer? That he is open, takes chances, dares to expose himself to the complexities of the enemy. That is what a writer should do. Not hide behind stereotypes—that's too easy; that's what the papers do, particularly in Israel and Palestine. So, say I was to write about this meeting between you and me, I would write about it from my point of view, from your point of view, from your wife's, from that of the three people sitting over there, and the suicide bomber who, right now, is walking down the street looking for a new target. Basically, I try to get under the skin of all these different people. When I write about the conflict, I write about our suffering, but it would not be right if I did not also try to write about how my friends, the now deceased Izzat Ghazzawi or Liana Badr [see chapter 10] or others, experience it too. I also have to include *their* justice, suffering, and mistakes."

One can honestly say that Grossman as a writer has tried to see the other side, not least in his nonfiction books. In *The Yellow Wind* (1987), Grossman meets Palestinians in the West Bank just before the outbreak of the first intifada, and in *Sleeping on a Wire* (1992), he documents his meetings with Palestinians living within Israel's borders. In both books, the Palestinians say, "The Israeli Jews do not see us. They do not know us."

I comment that that is the crux of the matter, that Jews do not see or know Palestinians.

"Of course, but I could argue the same about the Palestinians. After nearly a hundred years of killing, both the Palestinians and the Jews tend only to see the reflection of their own fear and suspicion. That's what my journalistic books are about."

"Would you say that the two books were a success, in that sense?"

"I think I made a contribution, however small and meager. *The Yellow Wind* sparked considerable controversy and did change opinions—for a while. People were forced to reformulate their arguments, something that hadn't happened for many years. I didn't offer any new facts, but I chose a new method, new words— something writers always do, by the way. A physical feeling of strangulation forces the writer to create new words, and when you create new words, it's like creating a new history. So the reader is caught off-guard, his old arguments no longer challenge what you're saying. For the first time in many years, Israelis were forced to see Palestinians as human beings. Of course, it was difficult for them, but at the same time they managed in a strange way to identify with the Palestinian suffering. I got thousands of letters from readers in response to the book, and most of them were touched and affected by what they had read. The book brought me into contact with many Israelis and Palestinians. As all the old arguments on both sides had worn thin, we suddenly experienced a wave of dialogue—for a short period."

"I understand that the prime minister at the time, Itzhak Shamir, had very strong opinions about the book?"

Grossman smiles, slightly embarrassed.

"Yes, he called it the imaginations of a fiction writer."

"What surprised you most during your research?"

"The depth of the Palestinians' frustration and depression. This was just before the first intifada and my main message was that the illusion we were living under couldn't last forever; we really didn't know what was happening out there, what we were doing to other people. Things were about to explode. And then, only a few months later, BANG!"

"It's now eighteen years since the book was published and very little seems to have changed—or has it?"

'Well, toward the end of the book I wrote that I didn't think that things would really change in the next fifteen to twenty years. I said that our own human stupidity, our inability to see reality for what it is unless we are forced to do so by violence, was a guarantee that the relationship between the Israelis and Palestinians would not fundamentally change. And I think that is still true of the situation today."

What happened next is well known. The first intifada erupted in 1987 and lasted until the Oslo Accords in 1993. So what about *Sleeping on a Wire*, which is about the Palestinians who live in Israel, not in the West Bank?

"I hadn't really foreseen how difficult it would be for an Israeli Jew to acknowledge the problems of Palestinians living here in Israel. It is possible, though difficult, to find a solution for the occupied territories, but it's worse for the Palestinians in Israel. People who were our deadly enemies in 1948 now have to share our Israeli identity and officially can even be elected prime minister. Not that they're happy here, we're talking about discrimination at many levels, but they do share the civic privileges, such as democracy and freedom of speech. At the same time, they're also forced to fund the repression of their brothers and sisters over the border, through taxes and rates. So the book generated considerable fear, people said that they would read it later, not now—and I interpreted that to mean that they would read it when reality forces them to. Many said that they couldn't feel any sympathy because the Palestinians here in Israel share the opinions of the Palestinian enemy in the territories. But the Palestinians here in Israel saw the book as a positive step."

Grossman's latest nonfiction work was published in autumn 2003. *Death as a Way of Life* is a collection of articles spanning the decade from the Oslo Accords to the present day. I see a clear downward spiral here. He started out optimistic in 1993 and ends on a more pessimistic note in 2003.

"Yes, I am more pessimistic now. I had a greater belief in both sides' rationality before and I thought that we were sick and tired of fighting each other. We *are* exhausted, but obviously not enough to stop killing each other. Both sides have become less rational and the fighting doesn't serve the interests of either side."

"Are they not able to see that themselves?"

"The problem is that on either side there is no connection between understanding and actions. I'm sure that everyone feels that they're living in terrible times. We know that the Israeli economy is slumping, that we have no security, and on top of that, we're now holing ourselves up behind that horrible wall, which will only mean that we end up living in a ghetto again. But it's difficult for people here in Israel to see the connection between the occupation and the terrorist attacks. They simply find it hard to comprehend that terrorism is a response to the occupation and that the attacks in fact correspond to what Israel is doing in the occupied territories. In much the same way that they cannot see the connection between our failing economy and the fact that we don't have peace. We know that the Palestinian National Authority is about to collapse economically, socially, and politically. None of us are enjoying life and still both sides are incapable of doing anything to improve the situation. Why? Because both sides have become paralyzed, which is usual in war, everything happens so fast, there's no time to think, to see the complexity of reality or to identify with the other side. Thus my sad conclusion is that a solution has to be forced on us from outside, in the form of massive pressure from Europe and the US."

Occupation in the Novel

Night falls over Jerusalem. A ghost town, says Grossman, where few people go out unless it is strictly necessary. The fear of more suicide attacks is paralyzing.

"Before, this café would have been packed on an evening like this," he exclaims. "But look at it now, only the two of us and those three over there, that's all."

The fact that there are not many people here puts me at ease. The fewer people the better. Normally when you travel out into the world, you look for the bars and restaurants that are bustling with people and life; lots of customers means good quality. In Israel, the opposite is true. Here, you go to the emptiest places because they're the safest. It is the absurd logic of the war here and something that has been learned fast: a suicide bomber looks for big crowds. That's just the way it is. I myself am staying in the old part of Jerusalem, which is completely safe. As much as possible, I stay away from Israeli West Jerusalem and in particular the main streets of Jaffa and Ben Yehuda, which have been the target of countless attacks in recent years.

The fear of suicide bombers affects us all: Israeli Jews, tourists—and Palestinians living in Israel. I met many Arab Israelis and they live with exactly the same fear as everyone else.

Grossman puts his coffee cup down carefully on the table. He has not only written about the conflict between the Israelis and Palestinians in his nonfiction books. His novel *The Smile of the Lamb*, which has been translated into Arabic and published in Ramallah, is about an idealistic soldier, Uri, who is serving in the occupied West Bank. It is about his wife; about an officer, Katzman; and not least, about a Palestinian storyteller, Khilmi, and his loving relationship to Uri. At one point, Khilmi says: "I love Uri, he is a son to me."

This novel is often mentioned when I ask Palestinian authors if they know of any positive images of Palestinians in Hebrew literature. I ask Grossman openly what he was trying to get across in this novel in particular.

"I was young and inexperienced, but I know why I wrote the book. I thought: how can it be that after fifteen years of occupation, there still is not one single Hebrew book about the occupation? And that is a good enough reason to write a book, that no one has written it before."

"The novel was translated by the critic Hassan Khander, and published by the Palestinian Writers' Union, on the initiative of Izzat Ghazzawi. I remember that Izzat once told me that he really liked the book and that he also believed in the Palestinian character, Khilmi."

"Well, I certainly hope so. If you write about a person, it has to be real. But I'm sure that if a Palestinian author had written about Khilmi, it would have been better."

"Uri, the Israeli protagonist, allows himself to be captured by Khilmi—in a way the two of them are in cahoots. The ransom is an end to the occupation. Would you say that Uri is close to you, in political terms?"

"Even when I write about Khilmi, a 75-year-old Palestinian madman, he is close to me. I can identify with all my characters. Parts of Uri are close to me, of course, but I'm probably a lot more pragmatic than he is. He allows himself to be taken hostage in order to change the situation. Well, that's a very unusual way of trying to change reality. It's a protest, in fact, because he *knows* that it's impossible, but he's so desperate. We're talking about 1982, and even then, Uri was so desperate that he chose a solution that is essentially a form of suicide. Just imagine what Uri would have done today."

"Were you a soldier in the territories yourself?"

"No. I was of course a soldier, for four years, in fact. In Sinai. As a solider, I was not very aware of Palestinian history, but I was very much a part of Israel's history. It was only after the war in Lebanon in 1982 that that started to change."

"What happened in 1982?"

"I was a soldier in Lebanon and started to ask questions like: what are we actually doing here? Will this solve the problems?"

The Other Side's Culture

Since 1982, Grossman has continued to ask critical questions, in both his newspaper articles and his literary work. For over twenty years, he has stood in the midst of the conflict in the Middle East and called for composure and peace. His great commitment surely must stem from a fundamental belief in the power of words? What does he have to say about the position of literature in Israel today? Do writers have any power or influence? What can literature accomplish?

"Literature functions as a kind of secular religion for many Israelis, and we read a lot. But is the author listened to? Well, I'm not sure. It is of course always fashionable to quote authors. But if people had really listened to writers like Amos Oz, A.B. Yehoshua, and Smilansky,[1] then reality would have looked very different."

"What about seeing *the other side* in your literature? Do you think that literature can play a similar role here in the Middle East to the one it so obviously did in South Africa?"

"I don't think so, because there is only a small trickle of literature from one side to the other."

"Yes, but could that change? In *Sleeping on a Wire*, you quote a Palestinian professor of literature as saying that if you live in Norway, you can possibly survive without reading Palestinian literature, but if you live in Israel, you don't have that choice. You *have* to read their literature. Do you agree?"

"Yes, I do agree, I absolutely believe that we should read Palestinian literature. When my Palestinian friends send me a book, I always read it. However, Palestinian literature is not the first that Israelis would choose to read. Perhaps because it places the blame so squarely on our shoulders. It can be difficult to confront the history of other side directly—the side that you humiliate, occupy, and are in conflict with."

In contrast to most Jewish Israelis, Grossman knows Arabic. Should Jewish Israelis learn Arabic at school?

"Of course. I myself had the choice, as a thirteen year old, between French and Arabic as a second foreign language, in addition to English. It was shortly after the Six-Day War in 1967 and my parents were truly shocked: 'Arabic? But they have no culture, they have nothing.' So I got out a huge atlas and pointed: 'We're here and Paris is there.' And it was the right decision. It is a sign of respect for other people when you make an effort to learn their language. At the same time you become more aware of nuances in their culture, see more easily what they are sensitive to, for example."

"But do you believe that the conflict has to be resolved at a political level first, and only then can literature play a role?"

"Yes, that is what I think. I have a feeling that the Palestinians are more interested in Israeli literature and culture than the other way round. And that is possibly because the occupied people are always more interested in decoding the occupier's codes than the other way round—in order to survive, but also to understand the roots of the situation. The Israelis don't really need to do that, not until reality forces them to do so."

Jewish Identity and Heritage

Grossman is known as a secular radical. So I'm interested to hear what Jewish identity is for him and what Jewish heritage, including the religious aspect, means to him, if anything.

"Yes, the Torah and other religious scripts are very important to me. After all, I am Jewish."

"So religious scripts are also important for secular Jews?"

"I am in no way religious. The only thing that I know as holy is the human being, life itself. But when I read the Torah or Talmud, I am immediately connected with a wealth of Jewish tradition and thought, the Jewish language, the Jewish way of perceiving others and ourselves, the moral issues. For me it is both a joy and a necessity."

"You mentioned the Jewish way of perceiving the world; would you say that there is a particularly Jewish way of storytelling?"

"Yes, Jewish irony. In a way, all authors are Jews, whether they are Christians or Muslims or whatever. What I am getting at is the sensitivity to nuances and human behavior and the ability to see reality from many different angles, which we like to believe is Jewish. The need to create abstract worlds is very Jewish. That is why we created an abstract God, the abstract worship of that God, and kept the notion of Israel as our country alive for 2,000 years in Diaspora. We have a talent for the abstract. And for surrealism."

"What would you say is the traditional Jewish attitude to the notion of the other?"

"Well, that's a very interesting question. There have always been two opposing impulses. On the one hand, there is a strong need to assimilate, to adopt the other's codes and even improve them—it's no coincidence that so many great scientists and artists have been Jews. On the other hand, there is a strong need to create a wall, to differentiate and separate us from them. That is, to be in contact, but still to maintain our individuality. I think that this has a lot to do with the fact that throughout history, the Jew has been portrayed as a kind of mystery, never just a person, but always a symbol of something else: the wandering Jew, the eternal Jew, etc. Both idealization and demonization are in fact dehumanization. The Jew was never seen as a person per se, but always as a metaphor. Zionism was an attempt to resolve this, to save us from this larger-than-life sphere and bring us back to reality, to have political organs, an identity, an army, agriculture, and culture. And if we now look back over the past three years, with the second intifada and all the terrorism, I would say that what we have witnessed is a growing anti-Semitism. It may be disguised as criticism of Israel, but Jews will always see it as anti-Semitism."

"From Europe, you mean?"

"Yes, of course. And from the Arab world. As a result of this, we see the modern Israeli, the one who thought he belonged to the modern world of the internet, cell phones, and MTV, suddenly being sucked into the traumas and wounds of Judaism and starting to redefine his identity in very Jewish terms: 'the whole world is against us'; 'no one understands us'; 'we are the absolute outsiders of the world'; 'we are seen as the symbol of all evil in the world.'"

Living after the Holocaust

I could not meet David Grossman without talking about *See Under: Love*, his great (in every way) Holocaust novel. If I were to point to one text that more than any other triggered my literary entry into the Middle East and thus to this book, it would have to be *See Under: Love*. It is a novel in four parts about Schlomo's journey from childhood to adulthood. He grows up in a suburb of Jerusalem, the son of two Holocaust survivors. Schlomo's great uncle plays a very decisive role in his life. The uncle was a writer of children's books before becoming a house Jew for an SS commander in a concentration camp in occupied Poland. It is this story that Schlomo, as a grown man and author, sets out to reconstruct. In my view, it is a prime example of the innumerable possibilities of the novel, stylistically, structurally, and otherwise.

"What were you trying to do or achieve with this novel?"

"The starting point is always to tell a story. A story about the possibility of living after Shoah, that is, the Holocaust, to love someone after Shoah, to have children when we know what people are capable of doing to each other, to try to be humane in a world that's so brutal. I had wanted to write about Shoah ever since I was exposed to it, and that happened when I was very young. I heard about the six million people who were killed and I was so shocked that I didn't want to carry on living. Later, when I decided to become a writer, I felt that I would never understand my own life—as a Jew, an Israeli, a father, a man, a lover, an author—unless I understood how I would have behaved there, in Shoah. And I wanted to write from two perspectives, from the Jew's, but also from the murderer's. It was crucial for me as a Jew to understand how I would have dealt with the total denial of my individuality and humanity in those conditions. But at the same time to try to understand how a normal person can become a murderer, what processes you have to go through to start killing. What do you have to deny inside in order to annihilate others?"

"And how do you feel today, did you manage to work through all that in your writing, in some way?"

"Yes. I think I managed to answer the questions I had. And I hope that I now know how to behave in morality's catastrophe zones. I like to think that I wouldn't find simple justifications for doing the wrong thing or allowing myself to see others as stereotypes, even when that is the easiest way out."

"The novel is also about storytelling's potential power. I'm thinking about the story Wassermann tells the German officer, Naigel, a kind of serialized story that continues night after night."

"Yes, as I write in the novel, the intention is to infect Naigel with humanity."

"And he manages, does he not?"

"I think there is something special about storytelling, something that happens when we listen to a good story—it reminds us of something we would rather not remember. Perhaps that's why people read less now than before, because it is a burden to read, it involves hard work and responsibility. I mean, to open ourselves to the complexity of the story, all the changes that a story *can* create in a person. It's far easier to watch TV or read the paper. Then you don't need to reformulate yourself the whole time, because basically the media reformulates the same story over and over again, generally using the same words too. Literature does the opposite: it forces you to redefine yourself, to identify with things that are frightening to you."

"I can see an existential view underpinning this novel—that being good is a choice?"

"Yes, I really believe that you don't have to work hard to do evil in this world. Ignoring other people's suffering and being indifferent has become a kind of routine. But if, on the other hand, you want to do good, you have to overcome your own laziness, your own routines. I believe that to win over this habitual behavior is to be human."

Grossman strokes his chin thoughtfully. Then he smiles: "Sorry that I'm talking in such old-fashioned terms."

"But surely there is still a lot to be learned from old terms and ideas?"

"Yes, of course, but I don't think that such ideas are very popular here in Israel. Maybe because of the situation. Or perhaps the situation has arisen precisely because we haven't made any effort with regard to these ideas and this way of thinking."

"Could it be that people find it difficult to understand Palestinian suffering because it always has to be filtered through the Holocaust?"

Grossman nods slowly.

"The Holocaust is still a bleeding wound, and it will take many, many years before we start to get over it. Because of the Holocaust, we have the tendency to interpret every conflict in total terms, as an existential conflict. That is actually very natural. If you have been bitten by the snake, you are suspicious of the rope, as one Jewish saying goes. After all, the Palestinians have been saying for years that they want to destroy Israel."

"The Palestinians that I talk to cannot understand why Israel should be frightened of them—they have nothing, after all."

"Well, there are 5.6 million Jews here, in the Mediterranean area. In Cairo alone there are 12 million Arabs. We live with the constant feeling that our future is very fragile. There may only be 3.5 million Palestinians in the Palestinian territories, but they are not alone. They belong to the huge Arab nation around us. Yes, many of our fears are imaginary and the result of past traumas and manipulation by our leaders and military forces. But we still can't ignore the fact that we are unwelcome here—and I am not now deciding whether that's because of them or us. You can't go to a mosque in the Middle East on a Friday these days without hearing that Israel must be destroyed. You often see people talking openly on Arabic television about their hope that Israel will disappear. So we have good reason to be frightened, we're not exactly surrounded by the Salvation Army."

"Perhaps part of the problem is that Israel looks to the West and not to its Arab and Muslim neighbors?"

"Yes, that's very true. Many Israelis consider the fact that we're here as some sort of bureaucratic error, because deep in our hearts we believe that we belong to Europe. And that's totally wrong, of course, because the majority of Israelis are in fact Oriental Jews."

"Yes, but the European Jews are still more influential?"

"That's right, but over 60 percent of Israel's Jews are Oriental. I think our wounds can finally begin to heal the day we truly start to understand that we are part of the Middle East, that this is where we belong. We could benefit in many ways from being a gateway between the East and the West. But it will take time, because we're not accepted here, as I said. But if there is peace, *when* there is peace, I think that Israel will be able to have access to all the great things the Arab world has to offer. Right now, we tend to see the horrific aspects, such as terrorism and fanaticism. But there are nearly a billion Arabs out there, so there will be plenty of opportunities to learn, be curious, study in Arabic countries and for cultural exchange. All this is possible!"

NOTES

1 Moshe Smilansky (1874–1953). Born in the Ukraine. He was 16 when he arrived in the then Palestine for the first time. He wrote his first story in 1906 (in Hebrew), which then grew into a series, and is also about the Arabs.

3

We have to act as if there is a chance. Maybe.

Yoram Kaniuk

It is a slightly disillusioned Yoram Kaniuk who welcomes me to his home on a beautiful, quiet street in Tel Aviv one day in April 2002. He is now 72, but still lithe and sharp, and his eyes twinkle when he smiles. His wife serves us coffee and puts some cakes on the table.

"So now you can write about how wonderfully hospitable the Jews are," Kaniuk remarks dryly, as he packs a pinch of snuff under his upper lip.

Kaniuk is in many ways an outsider in Hebrew literature. In the 1960s, he was already writing experimental, raw, and inventive texts when the rest of the country's literature was still wading knee-deep in social realism. He has been translated into a number of languages, but has never really become an icon in his own country. In spring 2002, however, *Adam's Circus* is playing to full houses in Tel Aviv—a dramatization of his novel *Adam Resurrected*, performed by Jewish immigrants from Russia. The venue for the production is a huge circus tent in the heart of the city. Kaniuk invites me to see the show one evening.

The performance is an amazing experience in itself, and afterward, Kaniuk is pulled into the ring, to rapturous applause from the audience. Even from where I am sitting in the back row, it is easy to see that he is moved. It is as if in this moment Israel finally embraced her uncontrollable son.

I primarily want to talk about peace with Kaniuk, as he was involved in peace work long before other well-known names such as Amos Oz and David Grossman popped up. As early as 1961,

Kaniuk was involved with what we today call the peace camp. He helped establish a committee for Jewish and Palestinian writers with, among others, the Palestinian author Emile Habibi.[1]

"When Arafat returned to Gaza in 1994, he wanted to meet the Israeli and Palestinian writers who had been working for peace for so many years. And what happened? Well, the Arabic writers didn't want to have a joint meeting with us and Arafat. They had no need for us anymore and didn't want to be seen with us. I met Arafat at the time, and he was very grateful for all that we'd done. I was more radical then than I am now. I met Palestinians illegally, did all sorts of organization work and was active in the peace camp right up until Camp David, despite the fact that I have always battled with my own doubts that the Arabs will never accept the Jews here. At Camp David, Arafat didn't have the mandate to say yes to Barak. He couldn't agree to a Palestinian state unless the Palestinian refugees from 1948 were allowed to return to Israel. And I don't believe that any other Palestinian leader will be able to do that either, not in the foreseeable future. So now I'm in a rather tricky situation: I want peace, but know that it cannot be achieved. The truth is that the Palestinians have the right to protest, because everything that you see around you was their country before 1948. But the problem is that we had no choice other than to come here because no one was willing to accept us."

So, after 40 years of working for peace, Kaniuk has lost faith— not just in peace, but also in the writer's ability to instigate change.

"I am not a prophet. I don't think that I know any more than other people just because I'm a writer. That's a myth, that writers know more or are better than others. Dostoevsky was a reactionary. Your own Hamsun was a Nazi. Both were great authors. I've realized that writers are normally wrong. Just think how many authors supported Stalin. Count them! The only one who was really against Stalin was Albert Camus, and other writers avoided him like the plague. We might be able to express things more eloquently, but that's all. I do still write an article now and then, but not very often. At 72, you get tired. I don't think it makes much difference anyway."

"What about literature, can that make a difference? Particularly in terms of seeing or understanding the other side, by reading their literature. For example, someone might read your own book, *Commander of the Exodus*, which is about the stream of Jewish refugees from Europe to Palestine after the war and, as you yourself wrote, be reminded of why Israel was established."[2]

"So why won't they publish it in Norway? In Sweden? In Denmark? Most European countries, with the exception of Germany and Italy, don't want to publish it. And it isn't a propaganda book that I've written. The book is about how the world closed its doors to the Jews, so that they only had one place to go. It does also contain some quite strong criticism of the US and the UK. It tells a history that has been forgotten, namely, this country's raison d'être, the story of why we had to have Israel. And it isn't translated, not because people don't want to know, but because they don't like Israel. I, for my part, like Israel, I want the country to get better, but I just don't know how."

A telephone rings somewhere in the apartment, and not long after Kaniuk's wife comes into the room and whispers something to him. He firmly shakes his head, he does not want to be interrupted, then looks straight at me again.

"Of course literature can captivate people, but the best thing would be to interview the books about their authors, not the other way round."

The Holocaust

Yoram Kaniuk's novels have been translated into many languages, but not into Arabic. This is perhaps slightly odd given that he worked so closely with the Palestinians and had so many friends among Palestinian and other Arabic intellectuals. Furthermore, his novels touch the essence of the Middle East conflict. Kaniuk believes there are very specific reasons for the lack of Arabic interest in his books.

"Most of my books are about the Holocaust, in one way or another. And the Holocaust doesn't translate well into Arabic, because they don't want the Jews to be right. An Arab author and good friend of mine once said: 'We suffered a lot in 1948, but when you come with the Holocaust, how can we even begin to compete?' And then it is better for them not to know. But one of my short stories and a good many of my articles have been translated into Arabic."

In Kaniuk's view, the Holocaust is Israel's raison d'être. And the Holocaust also stands at the center of his writing. But why?

"In 1948, soon after the state of Israel had been established, I got a job on the ship *Pan York*, which helped to transport Holocaust survivors from Europe to Israel. In this way, the Holocaust became my axis of rotation as a writer. I was the first person to write about Holocaust survivors, a kind of fantasy novel. The only way to describe hell is with laughter, to make it into a circus. The novel *Adam Resurrected* was published in 1968—and no one accepted it. The book incited terrible reactions and no one wanted to read it. That has changed over the years, but it took a long time. I paid a high price for that book."

Adam Resurrected takes place in an asylum in Arad in Israel in 1965. The protagonist, Adam, was a famous clown in Germany before the war, and he was ordered to perform as a clown and dog for the German SS Commander Klein in one of the concentration camps during the war. The novel is about the Holocaust and, not least, the (im)possibility of life after the Holocaust. And as an extension of that, it also deals with key questions of Jewish identity and Israel as such.

Conflict and Identity

Apart from *Adam Resurrected*, *Confessions of a Good Arab* is Kaniuk's most famous novel, a book that dives deep into the conflict between Israel and the Arab world. It is about 32-year-old Yosef, who looks back on and records his life. The starting point might sound like a melodrama, as his mother is Jewish and his father is Arab (Palestinian), but Kaniuk writes the story with unrelenting consequence.

It is about Yosef's split background and identity, how he is at once attracted to and repulsed by both the Jewish and the Arab. Attempts to draw conclusions from this very human tale would not yield much hope. With the Holocaust as a backdrop and his grandparents' flight from Germany to Israel, Yosef concludes that Israel was the necessary, if impossible answer to Shoah. And this is precisely the heart of the problem: that Israel was a *necessary* answer for the persecuted Jews and at the same time an *impossible* answer for the Palestinians who were driven out.

So there you have it: unsolved and impossible to solve. That is my understanding of the novel. I turn to Kaniuk, who gives a despondent shake of the head:

"I'm not very optimistic, no. Perhaps Israel will prove to be a passing phase in the history of the Jews. We don't have as much malevolence in us as we did in 1948. And we are too split, internally, with the religious versus the secular, etc. We are in the process of becoming weak. We doubt our own raison d'être. I really don't know if this can carry on much longer. It's a great shame, because I have children and I love this country and this language. We are stuck, surrounded by 250 million Arabs and a billion Muslims.[3] Arafat was very smart when he named the second intifada al-Aqsa, a name that existed long before Sharon's visit to the Temple Mount. He made the whole thing a *Muslim* concern. They will always attack us with the help of their religion, to make the struggle more attractive to the rest of the Muslim world."

Kaniuk is not frightened, he assures me, just sad, not least about having wasted so many years of his life working for a peace that—he now believes—does not stand a chance.

"You mentioned an internal split. Is it at all possible to talk about a shared Israeli-Jewish identity?"

"It was possible before, but that possibility has now been lost. We have given in too much to religious leaders. They have a lot of power in the Knesset, where they vote for more use of military force, without having to pay the price themselves, without having to sacrifice their own children, because religious Jews are exempt from military service. The Jewish identity is very complex. We have existed for some 3,000 years. We started out as a nation, then we were a religion, and now we're a nation again. And we still haven't managed to resolve the relationship between the religious and the secular. The idea of creating a Jewish identity was initially a Zionist project, with the revival of the Hebrew language as a key element. But that is harder now, when perhaps only half of Israel's Jews are Zionists and the rest are religious. No, fortunately there aren't as many religious Jews as that, but there are certainly enough to give them power. And many of them invoke God and settle on the West Bank, on Palestinian land. But we never saw this God in Auschwitz, he didn't step in to save millions of Jewish children back then, so why should he favor 2,000 fanatical Jews who live in the territories? Because these places are mentioned in the Bible? The point is that we're caught in the middle of a cultural conflict: Jews, Muslims, religious Jews, secular Jews, Sephardic Jews, Ashkenazi Jews, etc."

Kaniuk wrinkles his brow, puts a fresh pinch of snuff under his lips and ponders. "I don't know how we manage it, to live with so many internal divisions."

He confirms that he, like Grossman, reads the Bible and other Jewish religious scriptures, despite the fact that he does not think of himself as religious. He sees a fundamental difference between Jewish and Arab mentality.

"We say 'Peace Now' [the name of the most influential peace movement in Israel]. In contrast to Judaism and Christianity, Islam is about taking it easy. If you don't have money now, you'll get it later. If you don't get it later, your son will get it. If Arafat should die, they won't give up the fight, others will just take over. I have always admired their patience."

Wrong versus Wrong

While reading Kaniuk's novels I noticed many things, including the frequent use of the term "tragedy." According to Hegel, the main characteristic of a tragedy is a clash between two sides who are both right. And if that is the case, what is the solution? That will be the final and concluding point in this interview, as it is obvious that Kaniuk is starting to get tired.

"So, like Amos Oz, you are saying that this is a conflict between two sides who are both right?"

"No, I have always felt that it is a conflict between two sides who are both wrong. If you look at the political situation here in Israel, the real issue is that the left has never truly grasped the depth of the Arabs' hate for us, whereas the right has never understood anything other than force. So the tragedy is that the left does not understand the problem, but knows the answer. Whereas the right understands the problem, but doesn't know the answer. I certainly felt the tragedy far earlier in my books than I did in my political activities. This tragedy exists in novels such as *Confessions of a Good Arab* and *Adam Resurrected*. Deep down I have always felt that there is no hope, but at the same time I have always acted as if there was in fact hope. I learned that from Albert Camus, who once said that we have to act as if there is a chance. But now, I don't know anymore."

"With regard to Hegel's definition of tragedy: right clashes with right, but the end result does not necessarily need to be destruction. Could there also be room for reconciliation?"

"Well, it might still be possible to find a solution here, I hope so. But if that is the case, it isn't imminent."

"And to achieve that, the past may in fact have to be buried?"

"If you're asking whether we can live without a past, the answer is no. Both Jews and Arabs are far too attached to the past. But okay, if a real possibility of peace was to emerge in the next five years or so, then I would be so happy that I would willingly give up everything, even my memories."

Kaniuk smiles weakly and shrugs. "But I don't believe that it will happen."

NOTES

1 Emile Habibi (1919–1996) was an important Palestinian writer who lived and worked in Israel and was most famous for his burlesque

novel *The Secret Life of Saeed: The Pessoptimist.* Habibi was very active in the Jewish–Palestinian dialogue, and was also a member of the Knesset (Israeli parliament) for the Communist party for 19 years.

2 *Commander of the Exodus* is the biography of Yossi Harel, the man responsible for the transport of some 24,000 Holocaust survivors to Palestine in the period between 1946 and 1948. He broke the British blockade and smuggled them in illegally. His ship, the *Exodus*, "quickly [became] a beacon for Zionism," as it says on the book cover. In the forward, Kaniuk writes: "The state of Israel came into existence before it acquired a name, when its gates were locked to Jews, when the British fought against the survivors of the Holocaust." Elsewhere, the first Israeli prime minister, Ben-Gurion, is referred to as describing a tour of the European transit camps as "one of the worst experiences of his life." With intensified anger and helplessness and a pinch of regret, he repeated what he had proclaimed at a Zionist crisis summit at the Biltmore Hotel in New York in 1942: "Without a state, there can be no revival for the remnants of the Jewish people." This book is Kaniuk's attempt to illustrate what he told me in my interview with him, namely that the Jews had nowhere else to go and that is why Israel was established.

3 The majority of the world's Muslims are non-Arab. Indonesia is the world's largest Muslim country (in number of inhabitants), but it is not Arab. Countries such as Turkey are also Muslim but not Arab.

4

In conflicts, few people are able to understand the suffering of others

Amos Oz

Amos Oz is probably Israel's best-known living author. He has written over twenty books and has been translated into numerous languages. He is very active on the political front and was a founding member of Israel's Peace Now movement in 1977.

He lived on a kibbutz for 25 years, but now lives with his wife in the small town of Arad in the Negev desert. I wasn't able to meet Oz when I was in Israel in spring 2002. When I rang him, he asked me to call a few days later, when he might have more time. I phoned back, and he asked me to call again, and so it continued. In April 2002, the West Bank was in chaos, and Oz explained to me on the phone that he had to give priority to the domestic media.

But now, in October 2003, he welcomes me graciously and leads me down to his study in the basement. Various translations of his novels fill one of the shelves that line the walls. His novels span a period of 35 years and, in a calm and down-to-earth way, deal with many of the issues addressed in this book. The telephone rings several times in the course of the first seven minutes, with more than one journalist wanting to invite themselves for a visit. Oz is measured and polite: "Please call me again at the same time tomorrow, then we'll see. Maybe I can find some time." After the fourth phone call, he pulls out the phone plug. Not long after, his cell phone rings.

The last time we met was at the War and Peace Conference in Tromsø in early September 2001. The Palestinian writer Izzat

Ghazzawi was also there, as was André Brink from South Africa. I remind him of what Brink said at the conference, about the role that literature had played in South Africa.

"Could literature play a similar role here as it apparently did in South Africa?"

"Over the past three years, during this intifada, I haven't met Palestinian authors as often as I used to. But I'm in frequent telephone contact with many Palestinian writers and intellectuals. We often shout and argue with each other on the phone, but I've never had any personal conflicts with any of them. These are close relationships, very warm and intense."

"In literature as well?"

"Not directly. My literary work does not focus on the Israeli–Palestinian conflict. Let me put it another way: the conflict is *always* in the background, but *never* in the foreground. I don't write to compete with the headlines. A novel is about people, not about international conflicts."

"What about Brink's experience of learning to understand the other side through literature?"

"Unlike South Africa, the conflict here does not stem from a misunderstanding. It is not a result of Jews and Palestinians not knowing each other."

"Really?"

"No. The two sides don't know *enough* about each other, but that is not the crux of the matter. In the West, it's widely thought that every ethnic, religious, or international conflict essentially boils down to some kind of misunderstanding, so that if we could only bring people together for a lovely weekend in peaceful surroundings, so they could drink coffee together, get to know each other, realize that neither party has horns or tails, and perhaps add some group therapy and family counseling, then all the problems would disappear and there would be peace and love. But that is not the case here. The conflict is very real. The Palestinians see this country as their only one, and with very good reason. The Israelis feel exactly the same for exactly the same country, and they also have very strong arguments. And that is the basis for a terrible conflict. Rivers of coffee could be shared, but nothing will change the tragedy that two people actually have—not only *believe* they have—the same homeland."

"What is the solution then?"

"To facilitate a fair but very painful divorce. It is imperative to understand each other and do away with stereotypes, but that's still not the heart of the problem. The solution needs to be tenable for both parties, not just personal warmth, though that will follow, I'm sure."

"So what you're saying is the political solution comes first, then you can start to…"

"First, there must be two states so the Palestinians can have exactly what the Israeli Jews have, a country they can call their own, with all the security, dignity, and independence this entails, and recognition throughout the world. But also, within this semi-detached house, Israel has to be its own country, recognized by the Palestinians. Then the time will be ripe to knock on each other's doors and drink coffee together, to invite each other over for dinner. In South Africa, there was searing injustice between two societies in the same country, but here it is not just a question of societies, but states, and then we're talking about an international conflict."

This does not means that Oz does not acknowledge the potential power of literature, or that he is against translations between Hebrew and Arabic. On the contrary, in fact. And two of his novels have been translated into Arabic.

"My Egyptian publisher was severely criticized for publishing an Israeli novel. Quite a few of my short stories have also been published in Palestinian periodicals in the West Bank and here in Israel. And yes, I know that a considerable share of my work has traveled to Arabic countries and is read there. But not enough. Nor am I satisfied with the amount of Palestinian and Arabic literature being translated into Hebrew. But you see, here in Israel, it all boils down to commercial considerations: if a book has sales potential, it's translated. Every now and then a book might be translated for ideological reasons, but that doesn't happen very often."

Amos Oz has been a leading author in Israel for nearly a generation now. What are his thoughts on the writer's status in Israel?

"Most Israeli writers have been political doves, and many of them have also been activists. Not because they fully identify with the Palestinians in the same way that white writers came to identify with the anti-apartheid movement in South Africa. White writers there came to the conclusion that apartheid was wrong and the African movement was right. Mark my words, no Israeli author has ever said: 'OK, you want to know who is good and who is bad? Well, the Palestinians are the good guys and the Israelis are the bad guys, and the solution is for the Palestinians to take over!' That's not relevant in this conflict. Instead, various Israeli writers have said, in a number of ways, that we must be able to reach a compromise. Because this is not some Hollywood film about good versus evil, but a Greek tragedy where right fights against right."

"And in what way can authors help—if at all?"

"Novelists have some experience of complex relationships. As a novelist, you would never just say: 'The husband is a bastard and his wife is a saint, so the novel is about how awful he is and how fantastic she is, and the only solution is that she takes over.' No, your job is to see complexity. Sometimes to see both sides of the conflict, sometimes to play an extremely fast game of tennis with yourself, which is in fact what you do every time you write a dialogue. I think that novelists are practiced in taking this meta-ideological position, whereas politicians, ideologists, military people, and even ordinary people on the street prefer to feel that their side is right and that the enemy is wrong. The novelist has a more complex and tragic perception of the world. Sometimes I feel that it is difficult to communicate the inherent complexity of our conflict to those who are not involved, who often have their heads full of Vietnam and South Africa—conflicts where, from the moment you entered the arena, you knew who was good and who was bad. So I think that for us, here, novelists have had a very specific role, which is to inject complexity and to eradicate simplifications."

"And what about the Palestinian side, do you think that literature has had a similar role there?"

His cell phone rings. Oz shakes his head and gets up, picks up the phone without saying a word, and lets the person calling introduce himself, before confirming in his deep voice: "Speaking." A cat meows somewhere out in the dark; otherwise the world is completely still. This town, Arad, is sleepy as only small towns can be. I arrived here in plenty of time, so I ate a light lunch and then asked for directions to the address I'd been given. But neither the waiter nor any of the other guests had ever heard of a street by that name in Arad. So I mentioned that I was on my way to meet Amos Oz. That was the trump card. Fourteen people talked enthusiastically at the same time, pointing left and right. Of course they knew where Amos Oz lived!

He closes his cell phone, clears his throat, and sits down.

"Few Palestinian authors have been able to capture what needs to be reflected in literature, and that is complexity. But please don't misunderstand me, I am in no way judging my Palestinian colleagues and friends. It is harder for them, we are not on equal footing, it is *they* who live under a military occupation, not us. And what is more, they have never—not for a single day—lived in an open society. They didn't before the Israeli occupation, and they don't today, including those who live in Arab countries outside this occupied territory. Therefore it is much harder for them, not only because of censorship and persecution, but also because of their environment; certain types of readers who are not used to accepting just anything."

Like most Israeli authors and intellectuals I have spoken to, Oz regards Palestinian literature as being political.

"Yes, I would say that Palestinian literature, with a few exceptions, works for the political cause."

"Even today? Things have not changed?"

"Of course, there have been changes. I don't want to sound as if I'm accusing my Palestinian colleagues of being unable to see the conflict from both sides. As I said, their position is more difficult. Imagine that it was *me* who was living under a brutal military occupation. I'm not so sure that I would be able to describe the feelings of those wearing the uniforms. I'm not so sure because I have never been in that situation. But you're right, there *is* increasing complexity in more recent Palestinian literature. It is distancing itself more and more from political slogans, and the portrayal of Jews is less of a caricature."

"You mentioned that many Israeli authors have been and are politically active. A number of Palestinian writers have asked why, in the current situation, there are no protests from Israeli authors, as there were in 1982 when Israel bombed Beirut. Why are there no such protests today?"

"Well, in some ways the situation in Lebanon was very simple, but what is happening now is not just black and white. The point is that both sides are now fighting two battles at the same time. The Palestinians are fighting to end the occupation, for liberation and self-rule. And they are 100 percent right in doing so. At the same time, other Palestinians, such as Hamas, [Islamic] Jihad and others, are fighting to deny Jews that very same right. Israel is also fighting on two fronts, one of which is completely justified and that is the fight for existence and integrity, for the right to live. The other is to defend the settlers and the occupation of Palestinian territories. So, we have two times two conflicts, and this doubling is a source of endless confusion for the rest of the world, and for us too. And that is why I cannot speak out as my Palestinian friends wish, with resounding exclamation marks, and then march to the barricades. Because it is not that simple. At the same time, I don't expect Palestinian writers to shout and exclaim, 'Palestine stinks, because we kill Jewish children every day!'"

"Have you become more pessimistic over the years?"

"No. I have always been an optimist with no given time frame. I know how this conflict will be resolved, I just don't know when."

"Do you think that the leaders on both sides know, somewhere deep down, what the solution is?"

"I don't know what they think deep down. All I know is that the leaders on both sides are utterly inept at the moment. And it would not make me sad to see them go to hell, hand in hand."

Not a Good Theme for a Novel

Even 35 years after publication, *My Michael* is still Amos Oz's most famous novel. Personally, it is not the novel of his that I would recommend first, but *My Michael* is important in the context of my project, not least because of its portrayal of Palestinians. When I discuss the portrayal of Palestinians in Hebrew literature with Palestinian authors, they of course mention different writers and works, but none of them fail to criticize *My Michael*, in particular. The Palestinians in *My Michael* turn out to be terrorists, don't they?

When I mention some of these Palestinian interpretations of the novel to Oz, the author sighs.

"Misinterpretation of the novel is widespread. Because the truth is, there are no Palestinians in *My Michael*. It is true that there are two Palestinians in Hannah's imaginary world, but there are no Palestinian characters in the novel. They only exist as figments of Hannah's imaginary world. And for her, these elements express a combination of destruction and sexuality. They have very little to do with real Palestinians. The actual twins from her childhood could well be fat, wealthy, and well integrated in Kuwait today. I don't know, the novel doesn't say. The novel is about Hannah, not about the Israeli–Palestinian conflict. I am perfectly aware that I can say this a million times, and it will make no difference. People read what they want to into the novel. Maybe that is the author's lot when he lives in a conflict zone. No matter what he writes, it will immediately be interpreted as an allegory. People see headlines in the novel, no doubt because headlines are so prevalent nowadays. I hope that if someone reads my book in a hundred years time, they will not read it as an allegory for the conflict."

"Are you ever tempted to write about something that is totally unrelated to politics, simply in order to avoid political interpretations?"

"No, no. None of my novels are completely disconnected from politics. But nor are any of them political statements. If I want to make a political statement, I write a piece for the paper. If I want to tell the government to go to hell, then I write an article: 'Dear government, please go to hell.' They don't seem to listen to me, for some reason, but I still write it. I really don't need to write a novel in order to tell the government to go to hell, or the settlers not to settle on the West Bank, or the religious zealots not force their lifestyle on others, or the Palestinians to abandon terrorism. These are not good themes for a novel."

Zionism and Jewishness

The Middle East conflict is very much alive in Amos Oz's novels. The Palestinians are very much present. And the Jews, of course; Jewish identity is debated throughout his novels.

Etgar Keret described himself as a Jew living in Diaspora in Israel. When I ask Amos Oz how he defines himself, he answers: "I am an Israeli Jew, in that order."

"But Israel's Jews come from so many countries, linguistic groups, and cultures, so what do they have in common, if anything?"

"The Hebrew language. Israel is the only country in the world where this language is spoken, and language is not only your musical instrument, it's also part of your identity. A pianist is a pianist, a violinist is a violinist, they might be married and have a great time together—but they have different languages, and therefore also different sensibilities. It's a fact that it's much easier for me to communicate with a Palestinian who speaks good Hebrew—and there are plenty of them—than a Jew who doesn't speak any Hebrew at all. Because the language itself contains certain concepts, certain perspectives, attitudes to life, even a certain ethic. In Hebrew, the verb always comes first in the sentence. And you always say: 'David King,' and not 'King David'—and from this, certain priorities arise. He was David before he was king, and he will still be David when he is no longer king. So the noun comes before the adjective and the verb before the adverb, and that reflects a certain mentality."

"What about the Jewish and religious heritage in relation to identity, is that important for you?"

"Very. Just think that the Hebrew Bible is closer to today's Hebrew than Chaucer is to modern English. I am of course very aware of the vast Yiddish culture and Jewish authors who wrote or write in German and English, etc., but the greater part of the Jewish heritage is Hebrew."

"I am interested in how you see—or don't see—the other side. How would you say Jews have related to the other side, historically?"

"What is interesting and ironic is that both the Jews and the Arabs have been the victims in relation to Europe, but in different ways. The Arabs have been subjected to imperialism and colonialism, exploitation and degradation. The Jews have been persecuted, discriminated against, and the target of genocide. But the fact that both sides are victims of a common oppressor does not automatically mean that they love each other or will develop a sense of solidarity. Only in Brecht's plays do the suppressed march together to the barricades. In reality—and this is something that everyone knows—some of the worst conflicts often arise between victims of the very same suppressor. When two children who have the same cruel father look at each other, what do they see? They don't see the other one as a victim, but rather as an image of the cruel father. And that, broadly speaking, is the situation is here. So obviously it doesn't help that the Jews have a traumatic history. To expect Jews to be more sensitive to other people's suffering because they have a traumatic history is a sentimental misconception. Okay, we know that *some* victims do develop a higher degree of sensitivity to others' suffering, whereas others simply become more bitter, angry, and unreliable. Both these responses to suffering are very human, even if they are not equally humane. We have problems seeing the Palestinians' suffering because, in times of trouble, people have a tendency to see only their own suffering. This is a general truth: when a couple fight, they are both blinded by their own pain."

"If we look at developments in Europe from the mid-nineteenth century, we see a continent where a large proportion of the Jews were cosmopolitan, people without any particular home country, perhaps also without a specific language. What has happened to these cosmopolitan Jews?"

"Seventy years ago, my grandparents and other Jews of their generation were the only true Europeans; all the other inhabitants of Europe were patriots. So they were labeled cosmopolitans, which was the dirtiest word known to the Nazis and the Communists. As an intellectual, my father loved Europe and really felt he was a European. It is a sad fact that the world did not exactly embrace cosmopolitans, and that's also one of the main reasons why millions of Jews are here in Israel today. If the world had been more welcoming, a civilization without specific territorial loyalties, then the Jews would have flourished and shown the way. The current movement in large parts of Europe toward a more multicultural society came too late for the Jews. And it doesn't make the world as a whole a safer place for cosmopolitan Jews. I'm not saying that anything is going to happen to the Jews in Denmark or Italy in the immediate future. But I assume that if, for some reason, Israel's 5 1/2 million Jews were forced to leave this country, and let's say 200,000 of them found their way to your country, tolerance in Norway would be seriously put to the test. It might perhaps work with a couple of thousand, but hundreds of thousands has, historically, never worked—with all but a few exceptions. With only one exception in fact, and that is the US."

Amos Oz still describes himself as a Zionist. I knew this when I met him, so I was interested to hear how he would explain it. He shrugs and gives a slight shake of the head. Then he looks me straight in the eye again and coughs.

"That could take some time. I'll give you the short version. The problem is that people use the word Zionism, but mean totally different things. For some, it means rebuilding the ancient kingdoms of Solomon and David—I'm not one of them. For others, it means making an exact copy of the Eastern European *shtetl*. I don't belong to that group either. And for yet others, it represents the Jews' triumph over other people in this country— and I'm not one of them. For me it is very simple. As long as everyone on this earth for one reason or another has locks on their doors and bars on their windows, I think it would totally irresponsible of the Jews not to do the same. Not that I like bars and locks—personally I would prefer to live in a world with multiple civilizations and cultures, and not a single national state. Jews have for thousands of years existed without territories and national states, but I've seen what life is like when you're always a guest. Sometimes you're a welcome guest, and other times you're thrown headlong out of the door, while other people dance and enjoy themselves. So for me, Zionism is a security measure. The Jewish people, or at least the Jews who see themselves as a people and a nation, deserve a homeland. This right to territorial self-determination applies to the Jews just as much as it does to Dubai or North Yemen or any other country in the world."

"So two states then, Israel and Palestine, for two peoples?"

"For me, that would be an implementation of my inter-pretation of Zionism as a security measure. With two states, we could immediately start to work on a common market and maybe even at some point in the future move toward some form of federation, but not overnight. You don't jump directly from a deadly conflict into a nuptial bed."

"Can you really envisage some form of MEU, Middle Eastern Union, in the future?"

"Well, I don't want to make prophecies, but I will make one prediction: it took Europe a couple of thousand years and rivers of blood to get to where it is today. It will take us, in the Middle East, less than a thousand years and we will spill less blood. The first step has to be that the Palestinians are given what we Jews now have, a place they can call home. A window and a door that they can open and close as they wish. And if they invite me in, I would be happy to join them. And if they don't want me to come? Well, it's their home. It's that simple."

How is Zionism expressed in Oz's literary universe? *A Panther in the Basement* takes the form of a grown man looking back at his childhood in Jerusalem, where the action takes place over the course of a couple of weeks in 1947. Both his father and mother work for the resistance, trying to oust the British. I ask whether the book is also about trying to form a new identity.

"It is primarily a story about change. About changing stereotypical ideas about the enemy and the opposite sex. About the process that transforms a young boy from a chauvinistic slogan shouter into a thinking skeptic, within a couple of weeks. But the person who changes is seen to be a traitor by others, those who cannot change, who cannot even understand change. And the change carries a price: the boy gains insight, but loses his childhood. At the end of the novel, after the fortnight in which the action takes place, he is no longer a child."

"Surely it is also about the new Israel and the new Jew? But is it really possible to put the past behind you and make a fresh start?"

Oz shakes his head, thoughtfully; his cell phone rings again, he excuses himself, gets up and takes a few steps across the floor. I have to force myself not to listen, but cannot help hearing that this interview will be finished soon, in perhaps ten–fifteen minutes, he says, so call again then, Okay?

He sits down, apologizes again, and asks me to repeat the question. Then he shakes his head again, and takes his time: "The notion of being born again is pure sentimentality. People can of course change, up to a point. But when they change, they still carry their former self with them, inside. In short, it is impossible to draw a line in the sand and start a completely new life. There have been certain attempts, though. I don't care how successful these attempts have or have not been, because it is not necessarily essential that Israel forget everything that has happened in the past. It is perhaps not so bad that it deserves to be forgotten. You will find that the relationship to the past is complex in all my books. In the same way that you will find complex views on the conflict with the Palestinians and the question of identity. If I thought that I could put it all neatly into a small tidy drawer, I would be an idealist, not a novelist."

In my copy of the translation of *A Panther in the Basement*, I have underlined the following comment by the narrator, twice: "Our parents hoped that we children would grow up to become a completely new kind of Jew, an improved version, with broad shoulders, a fighter mentality, the ability to cultivate the land…" I quote these words to Oz, who rubs his chin and nods slowly.

"Well, the father is obviously an idealist who believes wholeheartedly in the various components of the Zionist vision: to build a new and just society, to find peace with the neighbors, to build a country without creating any injustices for anyone. This is a wonderful dream, but it is, unfortunately, very hard to realize. And that is, in fact, the case when we try to live out any dream. The only way to keep a dream intact and undisturbed is to never try to live it."

Fanaticism and the Holocaust

During his paper at the War and Peace Conference in Tromsø, Oz claimed that life had made him an expert in fanaticism, so if anyone needed a visiting professor in the subject, he would be happy to oblige. *Black Box*, which is perhaps his most successful novel to date, is to a great extent about the search for some kind of deliverance. It takes the form of a correspondence between Ilina and her former husband, Alec, who now lives in the US and is an expert on fanaticism. Together they have a son, and Ilina is remarried to the deeply religious Michael. At one point, Alec notes that humanity is in danger of destroying itself in its yearning for something higher. So is religion one of the main problems?

"The main problem is not religion as such, but fanaticism. And religion can easily, though not necessarily, mutate into fanaticism. But not just religion, everything can turn into fanaticism."

As he points out, I probably know many vegetarians who would eat me alive if they discovered I ate meat. Or pacifists who would happily shoot me through the head because my pacifism is not the same as theirs.

Oz shrugs and gives a weary smile: "What else is new?"

The interview is obviously coming to a close. But before my time is up, I want to ask briefly about Oz's thoughts on the role of the Holocaust in contemporary Israel and in Hebrew literature.

"The Holocaust will *always* play a role in our literature. Because novels and stories are always, in some way or another, retrospective, whether it's in the family or local history. So yes, I think that the Jews' collective history will always vibrate through our literature. But what I'm saying is actually meaningless, because it will of course resonate in different ways with different authors. Defining literature by one prevailing theme would be like saying: 'In Norwegian literature, there's a lot of cold weather.' And then what have you actually said about the literature?"

5

Dissension is an old Jewish tradition

Meir Shalev

More than a hundred years ago, Meir Shalev's grand-parents packed their belongings, left Russia and the Ukraine, and traveled to Palestine. Here they helped found the village of Nahalal, which was the first agricultural cooperative (*moshav*) in Palestine and a landmark in the history of Zionism.

Today, in spring 2002, Shalev has one foot in Jerusalem, where he has lived all his adult life, and the other in the village of Alonei Aba, a stone's throw away from his childhood home in Nahalal. He has a house in both places, but plans to settle in Alonei Aba soon.

In addition to his novels, Shalev is known for his radical statements in Israel's leading paper, *Yediot Aharonot*, where he has a weekly column.

I get off the bus from Haifa at the exit for Alonei Aba. I agreed with Shalev that I would call him from the bus and he would come to collect me. But the battery on my cell phone is flat, so I look around for a public phone. I eventually find one in a garish shopping mall just north of the highway. The heavily armed security guard yawns sleepily and nods at the suitcase in my hand. I try to tell him that I'm just going to make a quick call. He yawns and nods again. So I'm forced to open the suitcase and spread its contents out on the asphalt. A few items of clothing and far too many books. He nods, which I take to mean okay. Once I have rung, it's not long before Shalev appears. The lush Jezreel Valley shines green as we cruise along in his jeep and the air is fragrant with fresh grass and a thousand flowers. With great enthusiasm, Shalev points and tells me about one village after the next. He is a supple, light-footed man and his greatest passion, other than literature, is motocross.

The first and second emigrations from Eastern Europe to Palestine are a central theme in his writing. His novels follow families over several generations, with the action taking the reader up to the present day. Shalev is one for great, epic tales, with generous sprinklings of the fantastic, which has led more than one critic to compare him with the Latin American magical realists.

English readers may have come across *The Loves of Judith*, which has also been published under the title *Four Meals*, a family history and love story set in an Israeli settler village. It is about Zayde and his mother, Judith. The novel persistently avoids political realities and focuses instead on the characters' sometimes fantastic stories.

Shalev writes about the history of his ancestors, so I ask him to tell me more about his background and its importance to him as a novelist.

"All the people who set about building Nahalal were socialists from Eastern Europe. Both my mother and I were born in the village. My first novel, *The Blue Mountain*, is about the village, the myths and stories behind the legends of Zionism. It is not a political novel, it tells the story of a family over three generations. *The Loves of Judith* is a love story from the same village, and it is not about ideology either."

"Why are you constantly looking back and digging in Jewish history?"

"Primarily because I'm interested in the passage of time in a story, what happens to a family over time. The relationship between the parents and children, between the grandparents and grandchildren, love. The family is always central, I'm quite conservative in that way. I also feel that my grandparents' lives were much more dramatic and emotional than our lives are today. They burned with revolutionary zeal, left their homes and their familiar way of life, turned from religion to the secular, took personal initiative—what I'm writing about is basically the Zionist revolution. They rebelled against their parents and came here to reinstate the people of Israel in the country of Israel. Sometimes I feel envious, I would have loved to be alive then. They were also fantastic storytellers, and the family table was at the center of life."

Split Identity

I ask Shalev if he feels he has contributed to a kind of nation building, or if he is in some way helping to shape a Jewish/Israeli identity by constantly returning to its history.

"Yes, I suppose I have made some minor contributions to building the nation. Young people are often not very interested in the history of Zionism and things like that, but they become more interested when they read my novels, because I show it in a different light. A novel like *The Blue Mountain* is often read with great emotion and sentiment by Israelis, even very young readers. The book portrays the most significant period in Zionist history in Israel, though it is at times critical. And people get very emotional. But I have never set out to write a story in order to promote knowledge about Jewish history or the like. I write because I want to be at ease with myself, that's it."

"You say that your grandparents' lives were more dramatic and emotional than ours are today. Are you referring to the internal split in modern Israel? Were people more united back then than they are today?"

"No, not at all. Politicians in all countries, not just here, always say that the population has to be united in order to survive, but that's not necessarily true. The Jewish population has always been split, they have never been united. Even the Talmud is in fact a kind of debate. There have always been different sects, rabbi versus rabbi. In short, dissension is an old Jewish tradition."

"What about Jewish identity in contemporary Israel, would you say that it exists at all?"

"Today there are countless internal splits, as always. The secular versus the religious, who are internally fragmented in turn.

Israeli Jews versus Diaspora Jews. Zionists versus Orthodox Jews, who regard Zionism as a great sin. But I think all this dissension is a good thing. Great thinkers have always gone against unity, against what is accepted in contemporary thought. Take Galileo, or the prophets Jeremiah and Jesus—whom I see as a Jewish prophet—they all wanted to change the moral climate. The problem today is not so much identity—which is something that has to be felt, quite simply—but the lack of any form of spiritual authority, one that is accepted by all as a moral 'high court.' Today we have a situation where religious people do not recognize Israel's high court, and the various individual rabbis do not acknowledge each other."

"And there are Jews from many different countries, language groups, and cultures?'

"Yes, it's very mixed. When you say 'Israel,' you're talking about very different people. For example, all the Russians who have come here in the past few years. Are they Israel for me? Yes, when I hear their accent, I am very moved and happy, because they sound like my grandparents. Everyone here has their own ethnic group, depending on where they come from. I am actually a third-generation Israeli, so I have never really felt that ethnic bond before. But these new Russian immigrants have helped me to do that. Then there's my wife, who's from a Sephardic family with roots in Girona in Spain. I'm from a simple Ashkenazi family, and our children don't belong to either—and that is best, because then they have traditions from both sides [see chapter 1, note 4, and chapter 7 for more on the differences between Ashkenazi and Sephardic Jews]."

"But what is it then that binds the Jews of Israel together?"

'First and foremost, our very long history that makes us both proud and ashamed. And the fact that we are, and always have been, a people of words and ideas. We have never built pyramids or been great sportsmen, what we have created can be carried with you in a book or in your head. That's why we've been able to move around the globe so easily. And not forgetting, the Hebrew language. If King David were to walk in through the door now, I would in fact be able to talk to him. It's a completely unique phenomenon, that the Hebrew language has been resurrected after 2,000 years of silence. It was only used in synagogues and religious books during all that time."

"As a Hebrew author, do you feel that you belong to a Jewish tradition?"

"Yes, obviously. My language is bursting with biblical allusions, analogies, and metaphors—even though it is a modern language and not biblical."

"Would you say that there is a peculiarly Jewish way of telling stories?"

"I would say that there is a particular Eastern European Jewish way of storytelling. Lots of self-irony, self-flagellation, self-deprecation. I love that sense of humor. It has two main strands today, one in Israel and one in the US—just think of Woody Allen. Jewish humor in general is well known. As a Jewish writer you always have to be really good, because you are competing with a very long tradition."

There is a knock and one of Meir Shalev's nephews pops his head round the door to say that dinner is ready. I am the guest of honor. We have barely sat down around the dinner table—a total of five adults and two children—before the discussion develops into a loud debate about the situation in Israel, suicide bombers, the occupation, Zionism, Jewish identity, and who knows what else. I smile, watch, and listen.

After this delicious and very animated break, we return to Shalev's study, where he comments dryly, "What did I say about dissension? As you can see, there are internal splits even within families."

The Holocaust and Religion

The Holocaust is not really an important literary theme in Shalev's work, but it is still there, rumbling in the background. So I ask him about the Holocaust in relation to Jewish identity and literature.

"The Holocaust is still very much a part of the Israeli psyche and literature. It is not the main theme in my novels, true enough, but it is there, in the background, in the same way that it is the backdrop for each of us. After all, it's only two or three generations since it took place. But I don't like it in the least when Israel uses the Holocaust in an overtly political manner. Nor do I like the way that our education system emphasizes the Holocaust. Every year, our high-school students are sent on organized trips to the concentration camps in Europe. I want them to know about the Holocaust, but all the details? I don't know. I don't want to raise paranoid youngsters, I want to instill them with practical optimism. For me, one photograph of the Holocaust is sufficient. I cannot watch all the films or listen to all the witness statements— I would go crazy. I want my children to know the facts, but I want to be excused from that kind of emotional manipulation."

The Holocaust is problematic for Shalev, and so is religion, in every way.

"The conflict with the Palestinians is largely fueled by religion. That's what makes it so hard, because religion is an undemocratic way of thinking. When your politics are based on religion, it becomes very difficult to understand the other side. You have God on your side, so the others are inevitably inferior, and God wants to punish them. In addition, we have something that other conflict zones, such as Northern Ireland, do not have, and that is holy places. This complicates things even more. I, too, am moved by the fact that King David came from Bethlehem, but that doesn't mean that I have to own Bethlehem. That is the difference. There are also places in Jordan and Egypt that are important to us, but that doesn't mean that I want to occupy Egypt. No, you cannot go out to meet your neighbor with the Torah in hand and say, 'Listen, it's written here that all this is mine.' Don't get me wrong, I'm willing to fight for Israel, but the country's boundaries have to be decided on in relation to reality."

Shalev is therefore against the occupation and in favor of a Palestinian state.

"Just like a patient with a terrible disease, whose hand has to be amputated. You see, everything Israel has done since 1967 has in some form or other been connected to the occupation. Most of our energy, our blood and money are invested in the occupation. Let us rather reconnect to our heritage of words, ideas, and research. Such things are far more important than owning the patriarch's grave, the Wailing Wall, or any other holy place."

Literature and Conflict

Now we have come to the heart of the Middle East conflict, so I link together the two words conflict and literature. I ask Shalev if he thinks that literature has a role to play in the relationship between the Israelis and the Palestinians.

He wrinkles his nose.

"Not really. I don't think that literature has any real effect on the processes that take place in the real world. I express my views in my weekly newspaper column, as I did before I even made my debut as an author. From time to time, I sign a petition or make a speech at a demonstration—but I have to say that I'm slightly wary of all that."

"A number of Israeli authors write for the papers and most of them are radical, like yourself. What would you say about the writer's position in Israel in general?"

"Most authors here happily accept the old idea that we are relatives of the prophets because we also work with words. However, I don't think that I'm better than anyone else I know, either intellectually or morally. I make mistakes just like everyone else, even in my political pieces. I would actually prefer just to write novels and keep my mouth shut, and I'm waiting for the day when that's possible. You could say that the newspaper column has a practical function for me, in that it gives me regular pay. But I also feel obliged to do it, not only for my own sake, but also for my grandchildren. I want them to know that I did not remain silent when all this was happening. So I express my views, which is not always easy. Sometimes I'm shouted at on the street, for political or religious reasons. But still, I know that we are far more tolerant here than the Palestinians are, or Arab society in general."

"To return to literature: if you read the other side's literature, do you think that you could learn to see the other side more clearly?"

"Well, it's far more important to meet the people and talk to them. Literature is fiction, not truth, it's *supposed* to be lies—that's what our profession is about, lying. And what are authors, after all? The worst kind of dictator. Books are not democratic. We do what we want with our characters, we kill and do all sorts of things in our books. The only advantage of our profession is that that we have the ability to express our ideas."

"What do you think about the concept of literature as a polyphonic platform, the novel as a place for different voices?"

"You should talk to A.B. Yehoshua. He believes that literature allows you to get under someone else's skin. I don't know, I mean, we're talking about fictitious characters, not real people."

"And what about in schools, do you have any idea of how the other side is presented there?"

"Arabic school books are full of anti-Semitism. And I'm not guessing that, it's a fact. And stereotypes like the rich Jew, the blood sucker, the wandering Jew, the miser, etc. Jews and Arabs generally have very similar noses, but in Arabic cartoons, Jewish noses take on striking proportions. Our school books, on the other hand, are quite objective. They describe the Palestinian tragedy of 1948, and do not try to gloss over it. There was an incident involving the Israeli education minister last year [2001], when she removed a textbook from the curriculum because it was not Zionist enough, apparently. But generally, my children's school books look okay."

"What about the religious schools?"

"I don't know. But there isn't much bias in the state schools. As far as Palestinian literature in schools is concerned, Darwish has been introduced and some of his poems are very political. And the Egyptian writer Mahfouz is also included. Literature is generally given far too little time and attention in schools. Lots of people in Israel were angry when Darwish was introduced to the curriculum, for political reasons. I am critical, as a writer. If you only have two hours of literature a week, then *Moby-Dick* and Dostoevsky are more important than Mahmoud Darwish. Literature must not just become a little donkey that has to carry all these political issues on its back. You should study the best literature first, and then you can serve the political cause by studying Palestinian literature. Perhaps Palestinian literature could be studied in the history lessons, I don't know."

Shalev does not know much Palestinian literature, apart from Darwish.

"No, I have to admit that I'm not familiar with much modern Palestinian literature. I don't read Arabic and not much of it is translated into Hebrew. But I have read Darwish and he is a good poet."

"What about translation the other way? You yourself are translated into many languages, but not Arabic."

"No, but my newspaper articles are constantly being translated and printed in Arabic papers. Someone told me that a lot of people read my work in Palestine, and I hope that's true."

Portraying the Other Side

How does an Israeli-Jewish author portray a Palestinian? Palestinians don't play an important role in Shalev's literary universe, but they do exist. I'm also interested in some more general questions, such as whether writers are perhaps careful about what they write or whether they feel free to write what they think.

"What I'm afraid of is creating symbols. I don't want to have a single Arab or Jew who is supposed to represent an entire people. I believe that each person is unique. I want my characters to speak for themselves, in the same way that I'm representing myself right now, and not Israel or 'The Israeli Writer.' So I don't describe an Arab as 'An Arab,' but as a neighbor who is an Arab, and there's a big difference. I also want to have the freedom to write something bad about someone without generating the response, 'You're doing that *because* the person is Arab, because he is a Jew, black, woman, or whatever.'"

"If you read *The Blue Mountain* from a Palestinian perspective, you will immediately be confronted with the protagonist's parents, who are killed by a Palestinian terrorist."

"Yes, that scene is based on a real tragedy from my village, Nahalal. An Arab came and threw a hand grenade in through a bedroom window, killing a father and son. That was in 1932. In my novel, the event takes place some years later and the victims are a father and a mother. So I used a historical event, but that's not the only picture of Arabs in the book. When one of the Jewish boys from the village disappears, his Arab friends join the search parties. This is precisely the sort of relationship that I want to demonstrate—that the picture is very complex. Politically, there is great hate, but on a personal level, there are all sorts of sentiments and relations, including hate, friendship, etc. That's the reality, and that's the way it is in my books."

"From a historical perspective, what are the origins of the conflict and of the political hatred?"

"There are many bitter memories and a lot of blood on both sides. Not just in the past 35 years since the occupation of the West Bank and Gaza in 1967, or the past hundred years since the Zionist movement started to bring Jews back here, but right back to biblical times. God said to Abraham: 'Take your beloved son, Isaac, and sacrifice him.' But what about his other son, Ishmael, was he not loved by God? That's where the conflict started. It's interesting, because you find exactly the same story in the Qur'an, only there God asks for Ishmael to be sacrificed. You're talking about paternal love, and what is it that God really asks? That Abraham should sacrifice his *beloved* son. Personally, I hate the story, it's primitive and I don't want anything to do with it—but it shows us the roots of the conflict. We're talking about family relations that date back to pre-Christian times. We're not talking about one people that came from the east, i.e., the Arabs, and another that came from the west, the Jews—but about two people who grew up in the same tent, with one father and two mothers. It bears the seeds of a great drama, with all the complications that you can possibly imagine."

It's time to continue my journey. From here I travel east to Nasarat, where I stay with a Palestinian family for a few days, in a beautiful house where the parents stay up night after night watching the Arabic TV channel al-Jazeera. With deep sighs, they watch the images of what is going on just over the border, in the West Bank. From there, I travel to the Sea of Galilee and spend some quiet days in a convent, while Israeli military planes regularly scream across the blue sky. The nuns bemoan everything that the Israeli soldiers are doing in Bethlehem. Day after day, I wait in vain for the Israeli troops to withdraw from Ramallah and the West Bank, so that I can get in and find out what's happening.

A week later, the situation in the West Bank remains unchanged, so I return to Tel Aviv.

6

Arabophobia!

Orly Castel-Bloom

Orly Castel-Bloom is obviously very frustrated when I meet her in a café on the outskirts of Tel Aviv. Arafat is under house arrest in Ramallah, Israeli soldiers are annihilating large sections of the Jenin refugee camp, and Palestinian suicide bombers continue to blow up civilians in Israel.

"No security guards outside! No one checked my bags! This is madness! A suicide bomber could just walk in whenever he felt like it."

Orly Castel-Bloom is regarded as perhaps the most audacious, wild, and controversial writer in Israel today. Her novels are fantastically absurd, uncompromising, and pretty brutal, and the picture she draws of Israel is not exactly rose-tinted. When I met Keret, he named her, without a moment's hesitation, as his favorite Israeli author and used the words "universal genius" when I asked him to give a brief description. Kaniuk, an older writer, also mentioned Castel-Bloom when I asked him who were the most interesting young voices in contemporary Israel.

It is my understanding that Castel-Bloom is a writer you either love or hate. I have met more than one Israeli intellectual who cannot stand her. She has been translated into many languages and is particularly popular in France.

She sits down, looks at her watch and tells me that she has to be home in an hour and a half when her son gets back from school. We can meet again another day if necessary.

I open with a careful question about what she feels about her life these days.

"Life? This isn't a life. To know that your daughter is on a bus right now and then count the seconds until the bus arrives at school, to listen out for the sound of explosions. And she's at the rebellious stage. I say, 'Don't go there, it might be dangerous!' And she immediately goes there. My son, who is nine, understands the situation perfectly. After 9/11 he was frightened of flying, now he's frightened of people. Both of them have nightmares. I'm terrified as well, but what can you do?"

Orly Castel-Bloom has just published a new book, *Human Parts,* and the Israeli papers, including the English *Haaretz,* have dedicated pages and pages to her. She is in demand at the moment, but has managed to find some time for me. Her new book has been described as the first Hebrew novel to deal with the second intifada. And that is where I want to start, with an open question about why she wrote about that. Why write literature that goes straight to the hardest place and shows the darker side of reality?

"Well, on the one hand, I too have given in to escapism and have started to watch English-speaking soaps on TV. On the other hand, I have discovered that a very good way to deal with the situation is to write my way through it. I wanted to share my experiences with other Israelis through this new novel. At the same time, it is a protest against the media's total monopoly of the facts. The media is constantly on the move: to the next bomb, the next incident, the next statement from Colin Powell. Literature, however, can stop and zoom in on something interesting. This novel is also my first realistic book, and the first one that I have written in the third person. I am quite certain that what I see is what is really happening."

She nods thoughtfully, looks at me, then adds the small word: "Maybe."

I ask how has it been received.

"Well, not bad. Some grumbling that we get enough of that sort of thing on the news. I disagree. On TV, I saw that there had been another suicide bomb and they showed an interview with a man who knew his brother had been killed, but refused to believe it. At three in the morning someone knocked on his door. He knew it was the message that his brother was dead. He waited for about twenty seconds before opening the door. The TV reported this incident and then left him. And this is where literature can play a role, because literature can stay with him, explore the twenty seconds when he struggles with the knowledge of something that he does not want to have confirmed."

Orly Castel-Bloom knew the Palestinian author Emile Habibi, who died in 1996, but doesn't know any Palestinian authors living in the West Bank or Gaza. I try to find out what she knows about their literature.

"It's a good thing that Habibi is not here to see what is happening now. As for authors on the West Bank today, I can't read them because of the situation. I really feel that there is a barrier between us, and I don't want to waste my time. I'm so angry about what is happening here."

Meeting Israeli writers generally involves listening to harsh criticism of the current Israeli regime, with Sharon at the helm. Not so with Orly Castel-Bloom.

"I'm happy with Sharon. I'm not saying that he is perfect, but he is old and wise. The left wing here in Israel is far too naïve, particularly at a time like this. Not that I voted for Sharon, because my political position is pretty much in the center."

She pauses, searches for words and apologizes for her awkward English: "I have a dream; I dream that the Palestinians will calm down and learn to live in peace. But if that doesn't happen, I dream that they get their own state and kill each other, so that we are done with them. Because what do we actually want from them? Only that they leave us alone in peace, and stop killing us. Okay, I see Palestinians that have been injured and killed on TV, and I don't want any of them to die—it makes me sad. I can even feel sympathy for the mother of a suicide bomber when she cries. I don't believe that they are so ignorant that they do not grieve. But at the same time, I think to myself, 'They are the enemy, they want to kill you! So defend yourself.' And all the time there is this idiotic competition going on: who is the goodie and who is the baddie and who is right? Both sides are right!"

"What is the solution then, if both sides are right?"

"To split the country. But I don't trust them yet. First they have to stop all the killing."

"What about the Israeli killings in the West Bank?"

"I would not advise an Israeli withdrawal now. I know that people in Europe think that if the Israeli occupation were to end, it would put a stop to the suicide bombers, but that, quite frankly, is simplistic and naïve. I'm always unsure and constantly questioning things, not least what the true nature of the relationship is between Israel and the US. It is a terrible tragedy that we are so dependent on the US, but at the same time I know that we could not exist without them." She mimics Bush: "Withdraw from the occupied territories! I said now, immediately."

"But the Israelis haven't withdrawn," I argue. "So that must mean that you still have some degree of self-determination vis-à-vis the US."

"That's actually the source of great debate here right now, whether we should give in to pressure or not. None of us knows what will happen if we don't. Would the US actually bomb us? Would they stop giving us money?"

Literature and Identity

Interviewing Orly Castel-Bloom is unlike interviewing any other author. Her mind jumps around and she's impulsive, sometimes distant and at other times close. She can flare up, with sudden outbursts, only to be distracted by unspoken worries, her eye on the clock and her thoughts obviously with her son, who will soon be on his way home from school. For 99 percent of the world's writers who have just had a book published, there's nothing more interesting that talking about that book. But it would seem that for Castel-Bloom, reality has blasted a hole in *Human Parts*. I constantly have to force the conversation back to literature.

"You say that you don't trust the Palestinians, and possibly, the Palestinians don't trust you. But let's say that a Palestinian reads your latest novel, do you think he or she would be able to see and understand some of your life and your pain?"

Castel-Bloom snorts. "A Palestinian would throw the book away after reading two pages. I have tried to be objective and at the same time satirical—which is not politically correct. It is about our wretchedness and how we deal with it every day."

She frowns and confesses that she fears that what the world really wants is Israel to be wiped off the map. After all, what does the world actually gain from Israel's continued existence, when all that comes from here is bad news? When I then ask her about Jewish identity in today's Israel, her response is influenced by this perceived hostility in the world.

"What holds us together? The fact that everyone hates us. If Israel ceased to exist, if the Jews were annihilated, I think the world would lose a lot of good things: knowledge, good writers, good people with values. If people give in to their animal instincts, they will lose the Jews. What else binds us together? History. And our language. Hebrew is a very beautiful and rich language, and as an author, I feel that I am pursuing something important."

She believes that Kofi Annan, the UN, and Europe have exhausted their role and that they are too biased in favor of the Palestinians. She does not see any immediate resolution to the problems, and a ceasefire is all she dares to hope for.

"Let both sides bury their dead. Let the weapons be silent for a while. Let some months pass, maybe a whole year, before we even start to talk. There is so much hate, and the situation is so complicated. It is a bit like all the scientists in the world trying to find a cure for cancer together. So please: try to take part in this conflict between cultures without wiping out the Arabs or without killing all the Jews. In addition, people here fear the Jewish settlers in the West Bank and in Gaza. The last thing we need right now is that bunch of extremists coming to Israel, even though I think that will happen one day. Look around, this could be paradise! But we need vision, because just criticizing is not going to help anyone."

The Other Side

Orly Castel-Bloom's best-known novel is called *Dolly City*. It is absurd, burlesque, and perhaps slightly shocking. The novel is interesting, not least because of its unusual (to put it mildly) approach to Arabs and Palestinians.

One of many humorous high points is when the morbid protagonist, Dolly, opens a sort of psychiatric clinic without knowing anything about psychiatry—and makes a discovery. "I discovered a new type of phobia in Dolly City—Arabophobia, the fear of Arabs. I had lots of those sufferers. The ones with the compulsive fears, I harassed the most, because I read once somewhere that you should tackle your fear head on: fuck Arabs if you're afraid of them. You fuck them and you see that they're not such monsters after all; they're just like everyone else."

Castel-Bloom doesn't feel the need to balance the picture. In that sense, she is related to Keret; she writes about what she sees. And what she sees is a fundamental fear of Arabs. By writing about this straight from the hip, as it were, and not portraying any Arabs with attributes that could be described as human, she also provokes the question: is that really how Israelis see Arabs? Deliberately *failing* the other side in literature might be just as effective as well-intentioned attempts to understand them—if the measure of effectiveness is the extent to which the reader is drawn into the problem at hand. For example, throwing a corpse out from the 36th floor so that the hungry Arabs can eat it if they like is a concise and expressive image.

The text is so absurd, however, that you should be careful when trying to interpret it. In the blurb on the back sleeve of my English edition it says something about the character Dolly representing modern Israel. Dolly, who sees cancer everywhere— is it all a metaphor for today's Israel?

Castel-Bloom firmly shakes her head. "No, the novel was absolutely not intended as a metaphor."

She frowns, and is silent for a few seconds. Then it is as if she suddenly realizes something important: "Perhaps it *became* a metaphor, perhaps life made it into a metaphor. I invented a completely new concept, Arabophobia, and now it is a reality."

"You write about a development in the relationship between Jews and Arabs, which is connected to the shift in generations. As Dolly puts it: 'Yes, that's the generation gap for you, I reflected. My mother spits on the Arabs, I look them straight in the eye, and one day my son will lick their arses.' Should this be interpreted as some kind of prediction?"

"Well, I hope that it won't happen. I hope that we won't have to fight with them anymore. But the situation has been like this my whole life."

"*Dolly City* is undoubtedly your best-known novel. Do you think that it is received differently abroad than in Israel?"

"Generally, I would say that my work is seen to be more political abroad, particularly *Dolly City*. Foreign critics point out things like the mother's anxiety about sending her son to the army. Perhaps they're right, but it's also about being a sufficiently bad mother—which is what you have to be if your child is going to survive in this world."

Not Arabs

Orly Castel-Bloom is a Sephardic Jew, in the word's original meaning. "Sephardic" is derived from the Hebrew word for Spain, Sefaradh. Her paternal ancestors came from Spain. In 1492, all Jews—and Muslims—were exiled from Spain and many of them then settled along the southern shores of the Mediterranean. Her father's family settled in predominantly Muslim Egypt. They lived there for generations, until her father moved to Israel to live on a kibbutz, where he met the woman who was to be Orly's mother.

I ask about the influence this Arabic cultural background has had on Castel-Bloom and if she has learned anything from it. I am also interested to hear whether her parents spoke Arabic at home.

She shrugs and appears disinterested.

"They spoke Arabic sometimes, but behind closed doors, so that no one would think we were Arabs. I can't speak Arabic myself. We spoke French at home. I was three when I learned my first Hebrew word, so Hebrew is my second language."

"As a Sephardic Jew in Israel, have you experienced any kind of discrimination?"

"No, my mother was smart enough to use French for all it was worth, and she got us into good schools here in Tel Aviv."

Over half of Israel's Jews are Sephardic and have grown up in Arab or Muslim countries and their cultural background is overwhelmingly Arab. So I am fascinated to find out what actually happened to these Middle Eastern Jews when they came to Israel.

7

A perfect bridge

Dorit Rabinyan

Let me give you some facts about the population of Israel in 2004: around 20 percent of the country's population is Palestinian. Roughly half, maybe as much as 55 percent, are so-called Middle Eastern or Mizrahi Jews, that is, Jews who were born and have grown up in an Arab or Muslim country, and their descendants (they're also referred to as Sephardic, which denotes their religious rite). These people have grown up in an Arab culture, spoken Arabic at the dinner table, where they were served typical Arab dishes, not what we would think of as typically Jewish ones. You could say that roughly 70–75 percent of Israel's population has an Arab cultural background.

But the paradox is that the remaining 25 percent of the population, those with a European background (the Ashkenazim) have ruled Israel from 1948 to the present day. Israel has had twelve prime ministers from Ben-Gurion to Olmert, but none of them have been Sephardic. The Ashkenazim have not only been dominant politically, but also economically, socially, and culturally.

The leading Hebrew authors in Israel have been and still are of European descent. Amos Oz, Yoram Kaniuk, David Grossman, A.B. Yehoshua, Aharon Appelfeld, and Meir Shalev all have parents or grandparents who were born and grew up in Europe. The same is true of younger influential writers such as Etgar Keret.

I wonder, therefore, what happened to the Middle Eastern Jews in Israel and want to find out about Sephardic writers today, because they do exist, and Dorit Rabinyan is one of them. She was born in Israel in 1972, of Iranian parents who had come to the country only a few years earlier.[1] She has written two critically acclaimed novels, both of which have been translated into a number of languages, and both of which are about Middle Eastern Jews. Her first book, *Persian Brides*, portrays the life of a Jewish family in a fictitious Persian village in the early 1900s, whereas her second book, *Our Weddings* (in the US, titled *Strand of a Thousand Pearls*), is about contemporary Jewish family life in Givat Olga in Israel. Rabinyan's writing is vivid and sensual, physical and intimate—and at times, very direct and crude.

Dorit Rabinyan is a very likeable woman. She is intense, reflective, and humorous. When I listen to the two substantial recordings that I made with her—one in April 2002 and the other in October 2003—there is a lot of laughter from both of us. Between the two meetings, I began to realize how important the difference between Sephardic and Ashkenazi Jews actually is and that it is impossible to understand today's Israel without exploring this more thoroughly.

It is my last day in Israel and I am once again on my way from Jerusalem to Tel Aviv, cruising along at 120 kilometers an hour in a comfortable sherut taxi. Once again, I am struck by the statistic that more Israelis die in traffic accidents than as a result of the conflict with the Palestinians. It's easy to see that a good deal of Israeli aggression comes out in traffic. When we get to Tel Aviv, I wander south along the beach toward Jaffa, stopping for an Arabic coffee at the first café. The owner serves me in silence and then returns to his TV behind the counter. Later, I phone Dorit Rabinyan, who invites me over. Her sister is visiting from London, and the two of them welcome me with a smile. I open the conversation by asking straight out about what happened to the Sephardic Jews in Israel.

"Well, we prefer to be called Mizrahi, that is, Oriental or Eastern. The term Sephardic isn't used so much anymore, and actually refers to people from Spain. The answer to your question is one of the great failings of the Zionist movement. The movement started in Europe and spread out from there, and as a result, the hegemony in Israel is European, which is foreign to this region. I believe that the conflict in the Middle East is what it is today because the Mizrahi Jews who emigrated here from Muslim countries have been so passive."

"Passive?"

"They were persuaded to come to the new land by the European Jews. Most of them had in fact dreamed of it for years, but they never actively left their countries. So in effect they came here as 'guests' of the Zionist movement, and they groveled and apologized as they came. The pioneers were European, and the greater part of Middle Eastern Jews became second-class citizens, the proletariat."

"In other words, they were discriminated against?"

"If you came from Iraq or Iran or Yemen, you were accepted as a Jew, but at the same time suspected of being an Arab. You looked like an Arab, you spoke Arabic, ate Arabic food and listened to Arabic music—in other words, your cultural heritage was Arab. People questioned what and who you really were, Israeli, Jew, or Arab. So those people who could have been a perfect bridge between the Palestinians and the newly established Israel were instead discriminated against and mentally confused. They were not respected for who they were, and their important potential for assimilation here in the region was never realized. After all, we're talking about people who have lived with Arabs for generations."

"Is it correct to say, then, that the Middle Eastern Jews left their own heritage behind when they came to Israel and adopted the memories of the European Jews instead?"

"Yes. In our history classes, I never learned that I too came from a specific place. I sat in the classroom and learned the history of my classmates. As if I came from Mars! A non-place. And certainly not from a place with any history, or one that deserved to be remembered, that might in fact have something to contribute to the new homeland, the newly established Israel."

"I assume you learned about the Holocaust?"

"The Holocaust effectively spewed the Jews out of Europe. Nothing even close to similar ever happened to the Jews in the Muslim world. Seen cynically, it seems strange that the Jews who were in effect exiled nevertheless continue to look to the European lifestyle with great veneration and try to recreate it in their own homeland. It makes you want to shout: 'Listen, people, you could have created something beautiful here, if you had only turned your backs on those who killed six million of you, and instead accepted that the people who live in this region have *never* done anything like that.' I think that the majority of Jews who used to live with the Arabs were more peaceful, friendlier, more natural and humane than the European Jews. For example, the Sephardic rabbis in Morocco used to preach a pragmatic, sensible Judaism. Orthodoxy did not exist in those communities. Here in Israel, everything has become stricter and more extreme, like an echo of the Ashkenazi rabbis who had their religion influenced by a Catholic environment, where guilt and punishment were key concepts."

"What happened to the Sephardic culture here in Israel? Does it still exist at all?"

"It was given no recognition. The European hegemony was so strong that it suppressed the very idea that there might be such a thing as Sephardic or Mizrahi culture."

"But has it continued to exist in one form or another?"

"Behind closed doors, yes. In formal situations, no. But if we look back over the past ten years, there has been a dramatic change. Today, the notion that Israel is a pluralistic and multicultural place is more accepted. The very fact that my books and books by Sami Michael[2] are being published is proof of that. Now you can listen to Middle Eastern music on the radio, watch TV dramas about families in Iraq or Iran, and it is all mainstream. It has received the Israeli stamp of kosher, as we say here. So now we are basically 100 percent Israeli. But that is something very recent."

So, if the Middle Eastern Jews now feel that they are respected and equally valued as Israelis today, has this then changed their relationship with the Palestinians? Have the Middle Eastern Jews with their newly gained status and their Arab cultural heritage now lain themselves down across the River Jordan—or the Green Line—to become the bridge that Rabinyan mentioned earlier?

She shakes her head sadly.

"I have no problem seeing the Palestinians' perspective. They question why it is that most of the people who vote for the right in Israel are in fact Middle Eastern, speak Arabic at home, listen to Arabic music and cherish their heritage from Arab countries. And I think this is Israel's truly great crime against the region. In order to really differentiate themselves from the Arabs, the Mizrahi Jews have become as conservative as possible. To demonstrate that they identify themselves as Israelis and express how Israeli they are, they hate the Arabs and declare: 'Let's kill them all!' I mean, come on! If it were not for Zionism, you would still be considered an Arab. If it were not for the fact that the European Jews accepted you as an Israeli, thus robbing you of your pride as an Arab, Oriental Jew, you would not be so hostile toward Arab culture. And that attitude in fact means you are hostile to yourself, to what you contain, your heritage and what essentially made you who you are."

"Does this also mean that even Mizrahi Jews today are more Western-oriented than Eastern-oriented?"

"Europe and the West have a strange hold on Mizrahi Jews. They represent values that are respected, but still the Mizrahis' behavior and lifestyle is very Middle Eastern. They have created an eclectic life, benefiting from all the privileges of the Western world, including satellite dishes that make it possible to enjoy all that the multicultural world has to offer. And yet from all these possibilities, they select the few channels that are relevant to them, be they Iranian or Egyptian. Living in Israel means that you have the choice. You can live a totally European lifestyle, or you can live a life that is oriented toward the Arab world. Or the third world, if you like."

As an author, Dorit Rabinyan writes about the Middle Eastern Jew, be it in the then Persia or today's Israel. Does she see herself as a Mizrahi writer?

"Yes, of course. Some of my female colleagues claim that my writing is not feminist literature. And I completely agree, because it is human literature, written by a woman. The fact that I am a woman colors my writing. I am proud of being a woman, just as I am proud of being an Israeli of Iranian descent. I write from what is essentially me, and being Iranian is absolutely an element of that."

Honor and Superstition

I ask Rabinyan if these Iranian and Middle Eastern elements are reflected in her novels and if so, whether this implies that the gap between the Jewish and the Arab is in fact closing somehow.

"Generally, you could say that literature projects something about life. If there is no dialogue between the Jews and the Palestinians, you don't write about it, except perhaps as a wistful dream. But I really do see some interesting similarities in Hebrew and Palestinian literature, especially the literature written by second generation Mizrahi Jews and post-1948 Palestinians. The two have a lot in common, or rather a lot of parallels, as their paths do not cross and they never refer to each other. But they deal with the same subjects, the same set of issues. So you could say that we are on the same track, just using different languages."

Rabinyan's novel *Persian Brides* takes place over the space of two days in a fictitious Persian village around 1920. It portrays a minority Jewish community in a predominantly Muslim country, and focuses on two young Jewish girls. It addresses the position and role of women, and how society expects women to behave. The style is brutal and direct. I ask how she would describe the novel, as Jewish or Middle Eastern?

"*Persian Brides* is about a Jewish community, but that isn't what's most important. For me, it is an Iranian book. It could have been written in any language, but it just happens to be written in Hebrew because my parents decided to settle in Israel. I was born in Israel and Hebrew is my language, but since I have been brought up by Iranian immigrants, the core of my identity is Iranian. So I am a very cosmopolitan person, I have been educated within the framework of Western culture and I deeply appreciate that. But at the same time, I already carry with me the baggage that my parents were never allowed to open in public. The metaphorical suitcases that they brought with them from Iran were a large and important part of my childhood and youth. The differences between me and an author like Etgar Keret, who has parents who survived the Holocaust, are obvious—but so are the similarities. In a way, we are both telling the stories of those who were silenced by Israeli hegemony. There was a conformity that said, 'Let bygones be bygones! We will create a new country! We want the children here to be proud and magnificent!' But this is not a fair game. And there is a great opportunity for literature here, to give voice to those silenced voices."

Dorit Rabinyan herself grew up with a silent voice. She was not taught Farsi, her parents' language. But as an adult she has started belly dancing and has learned Arabic through the music. There is something unmistakably Arabic about her literature—among other things, the focus on honor.

Rabinyan opens her hands, shrugs, then laughs. "There is nothing more Arabic than honor and shame."

"So that is some kind of common denominator for Sephardim and Arabs, the concept of honor?"

"Yes, it's so prominent in the culture, so fundamental and deep, that no matter how far away you travel, no matter how radically you change, you will still be affected by it. I hope that if I have children of my own one day, I will be sufficiently distanced from these values that were carried all the way from Teheran to Tel Aviv."

"So these concepts are still very much alive among Mizrahi Jews in Israel today?"

"I'll give you an illustration. Even the grandchildren of Middle Eastern immigrants still have an accent. It's over 50 years since these people came here, the second generation speaks Hebrew, and still, the third generation has an accent. In my second novel, *Our Weddings*, I tried to talk about the more sublime things that the Mizrahi Jews are the carriers of today, such as shame and feelings of inferiority, the feeling of being second class. They don't aim for a new alternative, they do not become leaders or even owners of this country.'

In addition to honor, I note that there is a healthy dose of superstition in her novels, a kind of superstition that has very little to do with classical Judaism, but has more in common with Arabic folklore. She points out that superstition is something you cannot shake off.

"If you only have this superstition and no conscience in addition, then you're trapped in spiritual poverty. It's difficult even for me to let go of the superstition, no matter how much I want to. My parents *cannot* let go, because that is all they have. The alternative is far too frightening."

"And the alternative is to take responsibility for and control of your own life?"

"Yes, and that's a frightening thought, because there are no role models. So you feel trapped in this poverty, a kind of regression into the past. And the truth is that if you asked my parents, they would tell you that they wanted a future for me, that I would become Israeli, and not be an immigrant like them."

Palestinian Friendship

It is evening in Jaffa in October 2003. Earlier in the day I was in Ramallah and met with the Palestinian author Yahya Yakhlif. I shuttle between Israeli and Palestinian writers and intellectuals with a number of burning questions, but first and foremost the question of seeing the other.

Sometimes I feel like a messenger between two distant planets. But then I meet Dorit Rabinyan, and suddenly the whole issue of seeing the other side is grounded again. She has spent most of her time since we last met in New York—or Jew York as she describes the metropolis. There she met a painter and writer who was a couple of years younger than she is. His name was Hassan Hourani.

A Palestinian. Born in Hebron in the West Bank, raised in Ramallah. His family originally came from Lod, not far from Israel's main airport, Ben-Gurion. And not far from the Mediterranean. But they had to flee in 1948.

She talks warmly of Hassan and is more than willing to tell me about the special relationship they had.

Obviously, she didn't meet only Palestinians in New York; she also met Jews, American Jews. But that was not quite the same. I ask her why.

"Maybe it has something to do with being in touch with life

itself, not just principles. I can see that I share a certain heritage with American Jews, and therefore there is a theoretical sense of belonging. But when I met a Palestinian who grew up in the same climate, under the same sun, with the same attitude to life, I immediately felt a much deeper and more personal connection. Because we are both from the Middle East—and the Middle East is so dominant in my life that I feel a foreigner among all these American Jews who feel so close to me just because we're all Jews. I can sit with a Palestinian in New York, in snow and freezing temperatures, talking about figs and palms and the sea, the very things that life is made of. There are so many parallels in our lives. Not to mention our mentality, body language, and temperament. If you then add the fact that I, in spirit, have been an Iranian all my life, then there is an immediate identification with Arab culture."

At the moment, Rabinyan is working on a new novel and on a translation of the most beautiful children's book she has ever seen. It contains 40 stories with 40 illustrations by none other than Hassan Hourani.

"I'm translating the book from Arabic to Hebrew. I've also managed to persuade my American publisher to publish the book in the US. I hope that it will be published in lots of countries, because quite apart from its obvious potency in the Middle East, it's a very important and beautiful book for children—and adults. I'm really proud to be able to promote it as much as I can. And Hassan was very precious to me."

Hassan Hourani studied in Baghdad for three years, then lived in New York for a couple of years, where he met Dorit Rabinyan. Sometimes she feels that what happened is her fault because she was the one who suggested that they should both leave New York and return home. Which they did. She came back to Tel Aviv and he to Ramallah. One day, he illegally crossed over to Israel from Ramallah, and headed for the sea. He had dreamed about it, his parents had talked about it: Jaffa, the sea. He went for a swim—and drowned.

Rabinyan believes that Hassan will achieve special status, at least in the Arab world, and especially with the Palestinians.

"The book is about a young boy who travels around from

place to place. He clearly has the potential to be a role model for freedom and peace."

Night is falling and the sea is blanketed in darkness. Prior to 1948, Jaffa was an Arab town, and it still has a substantial Palestinian population. A car careers past in the dark.

"Bloody Arabs!" Rabinyan exclaims and laughs. "That was always a joke between Hassan and me. I called him Arab and he called me Jew."

Jewish Identity

In light of what Rabinyan has said about the discrimination against the Mizrahim in Israel and about Arab cultural heritage versus European, I ask her what it is then that binds Israel's Jews together. And how would she define herself?

"I am Middle Eastern. It was more or less arbitrary that my parents chose Israel. They could easily have chosen Los Angeles, as many others in my families did. I could have been anywhere for that matter, but I would always be *me*: an Iranian and a Jew."

"And the Jewish part, what is that?"

"Judaism is not something I practice, but something that I carry inside. Being Israeli gives you the privilege of including Jewishness as part of a package, part of yourself. You don't ask any questions unless you want to. I have grown up in a Jewish country and I appreciate that."

"What about Jewish heritage, including religion, is that important to you?'

"Not what we learned at school. But the literature I value the most is those parts of the Bible that I read through choice and love. I am proud of the Bible and carry it with me. I read it as literature, I don't worship it, but I see it as part of who I am."

I mention that I'm interested in the issue of seeing or not seeing the other and ask her how what she thinks about Jews' relations to non-Jews.

Rabinyan lights a cigarette and gesticulates passionately. Her sister leans forward to listen.

"Judaism is a cult religion. There is no evangelizing, newcomers are not welcome. Religious Jews cultivate and practice segregation at all levels. In terms of food, they separate milk and meat. Our weekdays are different. There are various materials that you're not supposed to wear. In fact, there are lots of elements from God's creation that aren't allowed—ranging from certain types of fish that you cannot eat to certain types of people you cannot marry. So it's a very isolated position, which means that Jews— wherever they live—often stick together and don't assimilate. I really wish that Judaism could be practiced in the way it deserves, that those who claim to be Jewish could show more respect for the non-Jews around them, for a start. The way I see it, thinking and wisdom are absolutely fundamental to the Jewish attitude. Judaism has been elaborated throughout more than 2,000 years of exile, but now that we've become masters of this country, taken by power, this wisdom has suddenly been forgotten. Look at Jews in Diaspora, in the global society, the fact that they're a minority makes them better Jews."

"Really?"

"Of course. Because they don't see their Jewishness as a passport. For them, Judaism is an obligation to be better people, they don't have a choice. Here in Israel, the Bible is used to suppress other religions, to control other people's lives, to kick people out of their home and subdue an entire nation. Just because you've had this book for so long, and then come back to where the action took place, you feel you can say, 'I'm going to use force, I call on the army!' We're talking here about people who demand land for spiritual reasons, and it's done in such a crude way. That's exploiting the Bible."

Literature as a Bridge?

Dorit Rabinyan is currently directly involved in Jewish–Palestinian cultural exchanges. What does she see as the potential role of the author in the conflict? And what about the potential power of literature?

"The problem with Palestinian literature in Israel is that so few of us know anything about it."

"Did you ever read any Palestinian literature in the course of your schooling?"

"No, they thought it would be more useful for us to read James Joyce than the literature of our neighbors. I think it is in fact an Israeli policy *not* to translate Arabic literature. There is a hostile attitude that is being transferred from one generation to the next. The truth is that we do not have insight into their personal and cultural life. We have nothing that can be used to bridge the gap. Literature could, of course, be such a bridge, because it helps you to see that other people are human just like us."

"You yourself have been translated into many languages. Do you think that your novels will ever be translated into Arabic?"

"That would be fantastic! But it is utopic to think that we'll ever see Israeli books in Palestinian bookshops."

"But there *are* Israeli books in Palestinian bookshops. If you go to the bookshops in Saladin Street in East Jerusalem, for example."

"Yes, of course, some political books have been translated, like *The Yellow Wind* by David Grossman."

One might think that an author like Dorit Rabinyan could stand up in her own right in her own culture, in Israel, and say or write something with some kind of authority. She for her part is glad that authors are no longer seen as prophets.

"The old role for writers was linked to nation building. The country was so young, and we needed someone to speak on behalf of the people, but today, the disparity in opinions is so great that no one can claim to hold the absolute truth anymore. I can't stand up and say that I know the truth. I feel confused and at a loss, like most people. That's why I practically never write newspaper articles. Nothing here is black and white, everything is shades of gray. Even my left-wing politics are fluid, because everything in society is fluid. I'm no Amos Oz, who's always ready to take a firm stance. I need someone to talk to me. Personally, I prefer listening to academics rather than authors, because academics analyze reality every day. At a political level, he or she is far better equipped to do this than someone who can write a love story that makes me melt. Authors are best at internalization, having empathy—an author who is good is good at a personal level."

"In Europe, Amos Oz is often talked about as some kind of modern Israeli prophet."

"That's because he can't let go of the old prophetic gestures. It's a nice role and he's comfortable with it, and maybe we need him to open people's eyes. Who knows, maybe it's just me who's cynical. But there's nothing prophetic about the rest of us, particularly the younger writers. Your horoscope can tell you more about the future than we can. I don't see writing as a kind of vocation or destiny, but as the only profession that I've mastered. If someone discovers something greater underlying it all, then I've been lucky. But I don't work an eight-hour day in order to deliver a message. I'm trying to find out something about myself, about my life, trying to control something in all this chaos. For me, writing is the only way to give order to my life. To earn a living by doing something that gives me peace, and that makes me happy."

She takes a deep breath, frowns, and then bursts out laughing. "I'm not saying that writing actually *makes* me happy, or that I *am* actually at peace or that I even *earn* a living, but writing is the only thing I can do. Yet I really do hope that I'm wrong. After all, I myself am contributing to the idea that understanding and cooperation may materialize. I work with the Palestinians, I try to communicate, try to be a part of the intellectual movement that wants to build a bridge. But walking on that bridge, or being a brick in that bridge—I'm not sure how much value that would have. I believe in the masses, in what happens in the grass roots."

Two States

Before meeting Dorit Rabinyan, I read one of the rare newspaper articles she has written, which was published in the *Sunday Times*. Among other things, she wrote that "Israel's collective consciousness, which was the cornerstone of the foundation of the Zionist state 53 years ago and which bound the immigrants from all parts of the world into a people, into a nation, is no longer our consciousness. This is the archaic, too idealistic outlook on life of our parents that arouses in us a concealed snigger at the Sabbath-eve family dinners. According to it, the individual has to sacrifice his own good, his freedom, his life, for the common good. This outlook has not succeeded in upgrading itself to a modern, sophisticated version."[3]

Does this constitute a kind of farewell to Zionism? And a transition to what? Post-Zionism?

"The concept post-Zionism stems from the so-called new historians who in the early '90s came up with new facts, new stories, facts that the nation builders had omitted from textbooks in order to foster a generation that was proud and prepared to join the army and die, a generation fueled by patriotic loyalty. Facts such as the Palestinians being driven from their houses and having to flee in 1948. These new historians were deemed to be very radical, they sabotaged the prevailing views of Zionism and Israel. I personally am a radical and post-Zionist, in the sense that I take into account the fact that what we learned at school was not the absolute truth. At the same time, I live here in Israel, and in this sense I enjoy the fruits of the occupation in 1948. But I totally condemn the occupation in 1967. Israel is my only home. I know that it is built on a crime, and I am willing to pay for that crime, but I'm not willing to let Israel become a two-nation state. I want two states for two people, and I want to see the refugees from 1948 receive compensation for the crime that gave me my home, but I will never agree to creating a joint Jewish-Palestinian state between the River Jordan and the sea. I think that would be a catastrophe for the Jews. I want the Palestinian community to thrive, but not at the risk of becoming a refugee myself. And I say that with the greatest love for those who disagree with me, the sons and daughters of the refugees from 1948. They are welcome to come here and live in Jaffa, just as I sometimes go to live in New York, or my sister lives in London. They will have full rights here, but not citizenship."

For a while, the two Rabinyan sisters sit closely on the sofa and discuss something in Hebrew. After a while, Dorit lifts her head and looks at me: "They will have their Palestine, their own homeland. In order to achieve peace, we have to establish two states alongside one another."

NOTES

1 To clarify: Iranians are not Arab. The official language in Iran (called Persia until 1935) is Persian, which is an Indo-European language, and not a Semitic one like Arabic. It uses the Arabic alphabet, however, but with an additional four letters. Many Arabic loan words have also been integrated into the Persian language. Around 98 percent of the population of Iran is Muslim. Dorit Rabinyan and I sometimes use the terms "Arab" and "Arabic" in their wider sense, meaning Middle Eastern or Muslim.

2 Sami Michael was born in Baghdad in Iraq in 1926 and emigrated to Israel in 1949. He has written a dozen novels since his debut in 1973, a number of which have been translated in Western languages, and one of which, *Victoria* (1993), has been translated into Arabic.

3 Dorit Rabinyan, "Young, Troubled and Lost in the Promised Land," *Sunday Times* (London) December 2001.

8

Life is much richer

Mahmoud Shuqair

In the spring of 2002, I criss-crossed Israel to meet and interview a number of Israeli writers. These meetings were exciting and interesting, but my project was so far very unbalanced. The days passed and there was little to indicate that the Israeli tanks would soon withdraw from the West Bank, allowing me finally to get in and meet all the Palestinian writers I had arranged to interview. At regular intervals I phoned Izzat Ghazzawi, who, like all the other inhabitants of Ramallah, was living under strict curfew. Outside his windows, Israeli tanks thundered up and down the streets, crushing anything in their way. "There's not much food left here now," sighed Ghazzawi, "and the youngsters are going up the wall." But he was ever hopeful; every time I spoke to him, he figured it was only a matter of days before the military withdrawal.

And in fact on Sunday, April 21, my last day in the area, Ghazzawi rang me at my hotel in the old part of Jerusalem. "You've got a chance now," he said. "The curfew has just been lifted, and the streets of Ramallah are teeming with people. Apparently they have started to open the checkpoint at Kalandia as well."

I clambered into a sherut taxi down by Damascus Gate, which filled up quickly. Soon we were off. "Do you think we'll get through the checkpoint and into Ramallah?" I asked the man beside me. He shrugged, with a faint smile: "Inshallah," God willing. The journalist demon in me had stirred, and I have to admit that I was thinking about what a scoop it would be to get in so soon, to take photos of the devastation and get eyewitness accounts. During my stay in Israel, I had sent regular pieces about my impressions and experiences to the Norwegian daily newspaper *Klassekampen*. These had been printed as a series of reports under the title "Voices from the Middle East."

This was the West Bank and new territory for me. It was as if someone had toned down the color, just sand and dust and gray buildings. Rows of crushed cars by the roadside, the work of Israeli tanks. After a while, the sherut stopped. We all had to get out at the al-Ram checkpoint, as no vehicles were allowed to pass. I followed the line of people and after a good deal of chaos, ended up in a taxi on the other side where the driver wanted ten US dollars to drive me to Kalandia, the next checkpoint. The taxi driver's face lit up and he smiled happily when he heard I was Norwegian: "The Norwegians are really trying to help us Palestinians, we know that."

He was not the first Palestinian to express these feelings to me. Palestinians generally view Norwegians favorably.

The Kalandia checkpoint is an incredibly ugly place. Massive concrete blocks form a kind of enclosure around the temporary counters behind which Israeli soldiers slouch. Heavily armed soldiers stationed on the ridge of the hill above the checkpoint monitored the whole farce: endless lines of people hoping to be let through. One by one the people stepped forward and put their bags and luggage down on a table several meters away from the soldiers. They lifted up their tops to show their bare torsos and slowly turned around 360 degrees to prove that they did not have bombs strapped to their bodies. Then they went forward and showed their papers. In this way, the line slowly advanced. Some people got through and were let into Ramallah, but most had to retrace their journey with heavy steps.

Finally it was my turn. I put my bag on the table indicated. Thinking that it was utterly ridiculous that I, a Norwegian of trustworthy appearance, might be taken for a terrorist, I did not lift my shirt, but obediently turned around. A soldier nodded, indicating that I could come forward. I smiled, tried to be friendly. The Israeli soldier held out his hand, waiting for my papers, but gave nothing away. In a calm voice, I asked if he spoke English, then handed him my diary, which was open at the pages with the names and numbers of all the Palestinian authors I had come to meet. There was also a printout of an email from Izzat Ghazzawi, where he wrote, in English, that he was looking forward to welcoming me to Ramallah. The soldier handed back my papers and nodded silently to the right. My application had not been accepted.

So that was that. I got into another sherut taxi, with all the other bowed heads, and drove back to Jerusalem. "That's the way it is," the driver yawned. "It all depends on the soldier's mood. Who knows, maybe he had a big fight with his wife this morning."

Maybe. Back in Jerusalem, I called Ghazzawi, who, unlike me, was not at all surprised that I didn't get in. But in the meantime he had set up an interview with Mahmoud Shuqair, who was waiting for me to call. I said goodbye to Ghazzawi, thanked him for his help, and wished him all the best. Then I rang Shuqair.

Mahmoud Shuqair lives close to East Jerusalem and was therefore not affected by the curfews and tanks that had been a reality in the West Bank over the previous few weeks. He is an acclaimed author of short stories. His style is modern and experimental, with a surrealistic touch. I had read and enjoyed his very short, minimalist texts before we met. He is also an important intellectual in Palestine, having held key positions in the Palestinian Ministry of Culture and worked as editor of one of the Palestinian cultural periodicals. He has also worked for Ogarit publishing house and has been on the board of the Palestinian Writers' Union for a number of years.

Following our initial meeting in April 2002, I met Shuqair again the same autumn at the Kapittel Festival in Stavanger, Norway, and again in October 2003, when I returned to Israel and Palestine for my second round of interviews. In the meantime, he had also become my contact person on the Palestinian side, due to the sad death of Ghazzawi, and by then we had exchanged many emails.

It is a gentle man who meets me at a modern café in Saladin Street in East Jerusalem. It's hard to imagine that he has spent time in an Israeli prison. But he has, twice in fact, and both times for a year. Immediately after his second imprisonment in 1975, he was deported and went to live in exile in Lebanon, then Jordan, and, for the last three years before being allowed to return in 1993, in Prague.

During this meeting, I want to focus on artistic freedom in today's Palestine and on the potential impact that literature might have on the conflict with Israel.

He orders tea and I have a latté. This is a European café, not a traditional Palestinian one.

Shuqair nods seriously. "I believe that literature does have a role. Absolutely. Literature provides a good opportunity to see the other side."

"When you read Israeli literature yourself, do you feel that you understand and even identify with the Jews' thoughts, doubts, and fears?"

"Yes. I've just finished reading Etgar Keret, who was recently translated into Arabic and published in Ramallah. I noticed that he is not bound by any kind of Israeli ideology, but is concerned with human problems, down to the smallest thing. Even when he writes about us, the Palestinians, I can sort of understand what he is talking about. It is not necessary to expect writers from the other side to be like you, you simply have to recognize and accept that they are *not* you, that they are somewhere else, in another society. And likewise, Israelis have to recognize and accept that I do not see problems in the same way that they do, that I am not them. Literature helps us to see the other side as individuals, like you and me, and that we both have a right to live."

"So Keret has been translated from Hebrew into Arabic. Which other writers have been translated?"

"Translations are a very good thing, and I fully support them. I was the editor of a cultural magazine in Ramallah for many years, and we translated and published poems and short stories by Israeli authors, among others."

"If I were to walk into a bookshop here in East Jerusalem and ask for an Arabic translation of an Israeli writer, how many I would find?"

"Not many. I found some titles in Cairo. The El Jahib publishing house in Amman translates a lot of Israeli literature, particularly political and social literature, but also fiction. In Israel, the small publisher El Andaluz translates some Arabic writing into Hebrew."

"Who are your favorite Israeli writers?"

"I don't read a lot of Hebrew literature, but when I get the chance, I like reading A.B. Yehoshua, Amichai,[1] and Amos Oz. I've already mentioned Etgar Keret. I try to find others as well. Yes, I have read some others, in either Arabic or English."

Shuqair has many Israeli friends and acquaintances, in addition to his colleagues. Some years ago, he was involved in setting up a joint committee for Israeli and Palestinian writers. They met once in Jerusalem and once in Haifa, and then that was that. What happened?

"We didn't manage to establish a shared platform, a shared understanding or concept of the conflict, so we chose not to continue."

No More Sentimentality!

Before discussing the current situation for Palestinian writers and the central issue of censorship, we have to grapple with the basics. What is a Palestinian? How does Shuqair define himself as a Palestinian? I also wonder how Palestinian literature relates to Arabic literature in general.

"Palestinian literature is part of the Arabic literary world and is definitely influenced by it. There is much in common. But when we write about the conflict with Israel, we are more precise and convincing than other Arabic writers—because *we* are the ones in the middle of it. When, for example, an Egyptian author writes about the conflict, it is easy to see that it comes from the head, not the heart, and therefore it feels unrealistic. There are also certain local elements, such as style and folklore, which make it possible for the reader to feel that this is Palestinian."

"Am I right in thinking that there were changes in Palestinian literature after 1994, when the Palestinian Authority was established and so many writers returned after years in exile?"

"Well, you would need a critic to answer that question properly. But the fact that so many well-known writers returned has meant that the standard of literature in the West Bank and Gaza has improved. The return is itself now a literary theme."

"And many old themes, not least living in exile, must have vanished?"

"Now they write about coming back, about how things are here, which gives something new to literature. Romantic sentimentality and exaggeration belong to the past and we have stopped crying for our lost country. We have become more realistic and mature. We're forward-looking and convinced that there is a solution. Apart from that, we write about pretty much anything, a chair, the moon, a woman, love—human details."

"You said that Palestinian literature is part of Arabic literature. What about Palestinian identity then, is there such a thing?"

"The Palestinian people are the most politically aware of all the Arabs, because of the tragedy and daily conflict. The majority are interested in politics and know what is going on around them. And Palestinians feel very deeply that this is their country. At the same time, they are part of the Arab world, and are also open to the rest of the world and what is happening there."

Shuqair points out that most Palestinian writers and intellectuals are secular and oriented toward Europe and the Western world.

"We are deeply rooted in secular and radical left-wing ideology. Most Palestinian intellectuals have an affinity with and are influenced by Western culture."

"Is Western literature important to you? Are you as happy to read Kafka as I am?"

"Yes, yes. And we believe in the humane values of Western culture."

"What about your Arab and Muslim heritage, the Qur'an and other literature, is that important to you?"

Shuqair thinks about it, looks for words and apologizes for his clumsy English. He chuckles that he has not spoken English since we last met.

"I only embrace things that are progressive and humane, and I reject the rest. I hate the reactionary element of that heritage and actively work against it. Because we mustn't get stuck in the past, we have to look forward. When I think of myself, it's not in terms of Palestinian or Arab or Muslim, as I actually feel that I'm no different from anyone else. I primarily think of myself as a *human being*—not a Palestinian or an Arab or a Muslim. I feel that I can communicate with anyone, be they in Poland, London, or Paris. There is no real difference. We are all human beings."

Palestinian Taboo

Even though Mahmoud Shuqair is basically optimistic about the outlook for literature and Palestine, he can also see the problems around him.

"Palestinian literature has really developed and matured over the past few years. But our society is weighed down by bureaucracy, the authorities, the PLO. I've been a board member of the Writers' Union for the past sixteen years, and there has not been a single election in the course of that time. That's not normal! They say that it's because of the situation. OK, we *have* got problems, but if you really want an election, you can organize it. And all this is reflected in our literature and cultural life."

"In what way?"

"The Writers' Union has stagnated. There is no dialogue among the members. There is no program, no creative atmosphere. At the same time, some intellectuals go along with the authorities and are not critical. But the writer's role is to criticize everything. Many of us work for the Palestinian Authority, and that does jeopardize our independence somewhat and prevent many of us from voicing our criticism or pointing out what is wrong with our society and the authorities."

Having spent many days in Ramallah with writers and other

intellectuals, the fact that so many Palestinian writers have worked or still work for one of the ministries continues to puzzle me. Shouldn't a writer, of all people, stand alone? I feel that it is imperative to understand why, so I ask Shuqair about the close relationship between Palestinian writers and the authorities.

"Because there are no other opportunities, no other jobs. And we can't live solely from our writing alone. OK, we have five newspapers and some of us work for them, for example, Ghassan Zaqtan. The publishing industry is hardly worth talking about. But I still believe that we have certain possibilities to express criticism within the system, if not, perhaps, fundamental criticism."

"What are the limits of your freedom?"

"I feel that I have a certain degree of freedom. Things are better for us here than in many other Arab countries, though not as good as the intellectuals would like. Certain political issues have to be avoided, and there are other things that cannot be freely discussed. For example, you can write about corruption in general in the Palestinian Authority, but you cannot give actual examples or name anyone."

"Would it be dangerous to do so?"

"No, not dangerous, but you would create problems for yourself."

During my (fruitless) hunt for Mahmoud Darwish all over Ramallah, I came into contact with the renowned literary critic Hassan Khader, who is editor of the equally renowned publication *Al-Karmel*, of which Darwish is editor-in-chief. Khader listed three Arabic taboos: sex, religion, and politics. I mention these to Shuqair and ask him what he thinks.

"Yes, that's right. We are not only oppressed by the political system, including the intelligence services, but also by society at large, which is even worse. There are certain reactionary values, and if you criticize them, you will be threatened. And we have a problem with the position of women, with talking openly about relationships between men and women and sex. So yes, what Khader says is quite right."

"What happens in practice—you send a manuscript to a publisher, and then what?"

"Well, first of all, we have never had stable publishing houses. But Ogarit has been around for some years now, and that has helped. Ogarit has a committee that reads through the manuscripts and makes comments, and these are then sent back to the author. It works well."

"And if the author has written something critical about religion, what then?"

"I have actually read a fair amount for Ogarit, and don't remember ever receiving such a manuscript. Every writer has his or her own internal censor."

"Even young writers know instinctively what they can and cannot write about?"

"Yes, I've also read work by a number of the young writers. Sometimes there are some small digs at religion. I was the editor of an anthology of short stories by young Palestinian writers that was recently published in Jordan, and one of the authors wrote about a person who dies, whereupon the narrator turns his criticism to God. I asked the author to tone down the criticism, so that the short story would have a chance of being published. My regular publisher is in Amman and has an office in Beirut. So my publisher sends the manuscript to Beirut, where there is no censorship. The book is printed and published in Beirut and then brought back to Jordan. At the moment, it is easy to get a book published this way in Jordan. It is quite different if you send the manuscript directly to Jordan *before* it is published. Then they read every single word before starting negotiations. 'We don't want this here, or this, or this…' But if you come with a book that is already printed, and it doesn't contain any attacks on the Jordanian royal family or religion or wild sex scenes, then they'll say OK."

"So you don't actually write about religion at all?"

"No, no. If you have even the smallest sentence that hints at religion, they'll take you to court. There is a case going on in Jordan right now against a Palestinian poet. And a novel by the Syrian writer Haidar Haidar,[2] which only contained a small sentence or two that might allude to religion, caused massive demonstrations and resulted in a court case against him in Cairo. An Egyptian writer was killed, and even the Egyptian Nobel laureate Naguib Mahfouz has been subject to assassination attempts by fundamentalists. There are lots of examples."

"The case against Salman Rushdie is undoubtedly the best known in the West. Can an Arabic writer risk having a fatwa issued against them?"

"If you're talking about being killed, no. But there is a fatwa against an Egyptian couple, both professors, demanding that they get divorced. Some of our leading thinkers are working hard to promote secularization and worldliness in our society. The fundamentalists believe that secularization is opposed to religion. To which the secularist response is, 'No, we are not against religion, we just want to separate it from the state.' We have come up with a new motto to try to help these ideas become integrated in society, which is 'Secularization that believes.' We're not against religion, but the fundamentalists don't have the right to stop me from thinking and feeling what I want, and to create a totalitarian state. We can choose democracy, a free system with parties. I think that there is a possibility that it will all happen, and it's the only way forward. Even the majority of those who go to prayer do not support Hamas or [Islamic] Jihad on a political level, but are far more pragmatic."

"The majority?"

"Yes. If you said, 'We want two states and an end to the occupation,' then they would say, 'That's good, that's what we want.' Most people don't talk about liberating all of historical Palestine. It's true that a lot of people admire Hamas every time they carry out another operation [suicide bombing], but only because they suffer under the Israeli occupation. If we had a separate Palestinian state, with greater wealth and hope, recruitment to these causes would slowly but surely dry up."

I mention a recent survey that showed that 55 percent of Palestinians in the West Bank supported the suicide bombings. Shuqair nods, but believes that the figure was even higher before. I tell him about my own experiences in Palestinian East Jerusalem, and how frequently Palestinians approach me and want to know what I think about the suicide bombings. And I always tell them the truth, that I condemn them, that the Palestinians have a good and just cause, but that doesn't give them the right to take civilians' lives. The response to this worries me. Young men of around twenty or elderly shopkeepers of around sixty reply: "That's exactly what I thought before, but now..." "If someone came along and killed your wife and children and then tore down your house, what would you do then?" a gentle old man asks me. I constantly hear this sort of thing on the street and in the cafés. A steady stream of new Israeli military operations, a disastrous economy, the security wall, more and more checkpoints—all this has led to a change in the mentality of so-called normal people. And even though I am weary of expressions like "cycle of violence," this cycle is obviously happening right in front of me.

With regard to sex as a taboo, it is interesting to remember that in the Middle Ages, the golden age of Arabic culture, eroticism blossomed in literature. And Islam was as dominant then as it is now. I ask whether it is Islam that has changed.

Shuqair nods: "Yes, of course. And it's true, there were many books about sex in the Middle Ages, they were famous, and there were no problems about it. Take *A Thousand and One Nights*, it's full of sex. However, you should remember that the books were really only for the elite in those days, and the masses, as such, didn't really know or bother about them. But the main point is that Islam was different then, it was more tolerant. Under the rule of the Abbasids [750–1258], culture blossomed and there were many philosophers and writers. Today, however, we are governed by other traditions. And these traditions are not true Islam, in fact, they are alien to Islam."

When I ask, more specifically, what has happened to Islam and what caused this change, Shuqair lists a great number of things. Defeat in the Six-Day War in 1967. The Israeli occupation. The Iranian revolution. A failing economy.

"And the support that the Arab world got from the CIA and the US to act as a buffer against communism. The reactionary

Arabic regimes used increasingly religious propaganda to fight against communism and the left in general. They forced more and more religion on schools and universities. All these factors play a part. So, even though the West has democratic values, people started to think, 'How can I believe in these values when they still want kill me? No, I have to go back to my own roots, to religion.' But as I said, if there were more realistic and concrete steps toward peace, giving justified hope for the future, fundamentalism would diminish."

Political Pathos

Palestinian literature is political and full of pathos. Again and again I hear this description, and not just from Israelis. But is it really true?

Shuqair's short stories were written over a period of around 40 years and clearly demonstrate that he has undergone great changes as a writer. I ask whether he could be used as an example to illustrate the development of Palestinian literature in general.

"Yes. Before, our literature was certainly characterized by confrontation and opposition. But now the perspective is much broader. Some more recent Palestinian literature opens the way for dialogue, to discuss the conflict, and that is something new. I myself have written a novel for young people about a meeting between a Palestinian boy and an Israeli girl on a bus. The two of them get off the bus together. He is on his way to his grandfather's house, which they then discover is her house now. The ending is not exactly a *happy* one, but opens up for reflections on this complex situation. It is *possible* to develop a relationship. But with the occupation, it's very difficult. You'll also find that some of our modern literature praises the struggle for peace in Israel. I wrote a short story about the famous Israeli lawyer Felicia Langer,[3] who was my lawyer when I was in prison. She later moved to Germany because she was being threatened. I wrote a story about her visiting a Palestinian boy in prison; she embraces him and breast-feeds him, and the officers who are watching go crazy."

Shuqair laughs out loud, sips his tea, and searches for right words. "It is a symbolic story. Certainly, I always used to focus on the Palestinian tragedy and all my short stories were about that. Today, I write in a more humane style. If it is included at all, the political situation is more of a backdrop in my stories. If I write about the problems, I approach them from a human angle. But I have to say, because there is still no solution to the tragedy, it is difficult for Palestinian authors to avoid writing about the situation in one way or another. If there were no conflict, writers would have more opportunities. We don't want to continue writing about the conflict, because life is much richer than that."

"If we look back through Palestinian literature, would we find a succession of books about political issues and the difficulties of living in exile?"

"Yes, but life in exile *is* difficult. We're talking about Palestinians who were deported from their country and live in camps all over the place, as refugees. Because Palestinians have been oppressed for so many years, the writer wanted to awaken the reader's national pride by talking about the homeland."

"How would you say that the Palestinian is traditionally portrayed in Palestinian literature—as the victim?"

"Yes, because they are also victims in reality. And if you ask how the other side is portrayed, well, the majority of Palestinian writers today see Israelis as normal people, with the same right to life as us."

"Is that also reflected in Palestinian literature, the fact that Jews are ordinary people, not just soldiers?"

"Yes. The conflict has gone on for so long that many opinions have changed along the way, become more realistic, more human. We are victims, but we also take into account the Jews' suffering during the war, when they were Hitler's victims. It is true that our image of the Jews was at best unclear before 1967, and at worst full of unrealistic details. At the time, for example, Egyptian films portrayed Jews as being stingy, dishonest, and conspiratorial rogues, but that is not the case today. There is no stereotypical image of the Jew anymore."

Humanity

The Homeland is a challenging, dreamlike and in part surrealistic short story about a Palestinian man who is standing studying the city wall of his home town when an Israeli soldier approaches him and sneers: "This, your city? Rubbish!" The protagonist pulls out a knife and kills the soldier, and is subsequently thrown into prison, then forced to leave the country. A series of scenes from Beirut follows, before the protagonist meets an armed *fedayeen* (resistance fighter) and, with him, marches toward the homeland.

The short story was written in 1975, just after Shuqair himself had been deported to Lebanon.

"This story belongs to your earlier, political writing, right?"

"Yes. I am not keen on that kind of literature anymore. It's a story that promotes armed opposition."

"Would you say that it's a fairly typical piece of Palestinian writing from the mid-1970s?"

"Yes. I don't write like that anymore. At the time, I had just been deported from my country, was living in exile and life in Beirut during the civil war was not easy. So in a way, I wanted revenge on the occupying forces: we must fight against them!"

"A kind of mini-autobiography?"

"Yes. And a story about resistance. At the time, our most important role as writers was to oppose the occupation and return home."

"Do you still like the short story when you read it now, thirty years on?"

"Yes. I like the story, but not the ending, not the fact that there is only one solution. Today I feel that life is richer and that opens the way for more possibilities in literature."

Shuqair in fact wrote short stories in the 1960s that were richer, as he puts it—that is, more humane and less political. What happened? He thinks for a long time, grabs hold of a passing waiter and orders two glasses of juice. An acquaintance comes in and greets him, and says hello to me before moving on. The juice is served in tall, slim glasses with ice cubes, straws, and an umbrella to top it off. Shuqair takes a sip and coughs.

"In those days, I was still not a political person. I used to write from my innermost emotions. Well, I made a mistake in the mid-1970s and dragged it into the 1980s. I let my writing serve my political cause. If you have an idea in your head and want to write a story, that idea can quickly ruin the story. You have to give the story a chance to develop by itself."

"What was it that made you less political again?"

Again, he thinks for a while before answering: "The collapse of the Soviet Union. I was in the central committee of the Palestinian communist party. My understanding of socialism, Marxism, and the Eastern Bloc was influenced by Soviet thinking. I later understood—as did many others—that this was not positive, rather it was narrow-minded. I was also inspired by Marxist critics at the time, people who claimed that art and literature should promote revolution." He gives a short burst of laughter, before continuing: "I wrote a television series and it was the biggest catastrophe of my life. The series was bursting with politics and ideology. The collapse of the Soviet Union helped me to liberate my literature from political and ideological obligations. Today, I try constantly to renew my views, change my opinions, in short, I try not to be who I was twenty years ago."

Since then, Shuqair has published three collections of prose. He was the first Palestinian to write in this genre. The texts are snapshots of life, devoid of politics, and are about human issues such as loneliness and poverty.[4] *Things* is seven-and-a-half lines long and describes how a woman uses all her wages to buy medicine for her husband, clothes for her daughter, notebooks for her boys and, for the first time in her life, makeup and perfume for herself.

Shuqair's most recent publication, a collection of short stories from 2003, is part of this new era. The stories look at the conflict between the older generation on the one hand and modernity on the other. In "Ronaldo's Seat," the taxi driver Kathem Ali has exchanged emails with the famous Brazilian soccer player Ronaldo, and starts to tell people that Ronaldo is coming soon. No one is allowed to sit in the passenger seat of his taxi, because it is reserved for Ronaldo. Even though everyone knows that Kathem loves his wife, rumors start to spread that the seat is in fact reserved for clandestine meetings with other women. Kathem has to pay the price of these rumors and is beaten up by masked men.

There is a tension between the dreams we nurture, and gossip. The story illustrates the split between traditional values and modernity in contemporary Palestine.

Shuqair's light surrealistic touch enables you to read his short stories as both realistic and unrealistic at the same time. Perhaps it is precisely this ambiguity that makes it possible to touch upon more inflammatory subjects.

I turn to Shuqair with one final question. "What are you striving to achieve as a writer?"

"That's a big question. First and foremost, I like writing. I feel that writing is essential to me as a person. Money is not that important to me. The most important thing is to make life meaningful. When I write, I feel balanced, and I feel that I have a role to play. I like to pursue human weakness and write about it. Despite our weaknesses, we live and carry out our mission in life. Such is life. People have the capacity for both good and evil. We have our hopes, but still at times feel that life is not worth living. When literature evokes such human emotions, I think it can make life easier."

Notes

1 Yehuda Amichai (1924–2000) is Israel's best-known poet. He was born in Würzburg, Germany, and grew up in an Orthodox Jewish environment. He moved to Palestine in 1935. He has written two novels, a collection of short stories, some children's books and plays, but is best known as a poet. He has been translated into 33 languages.

2 Haidar Haidar (born 1936). The novel, *Banquet for Seaweed*, which has not been translated, unleashed a storm when it was republished in Cairo twenty years after its original publication. For more about Haidar and the controversy concerning this novel, see Hafez (2000).

3 Felicia Langer (born 1948) moved to Israel from Poland in 1950 and lived there until 1990, when she settled in Germany. She became

very involved in the Palestinian cause, particularly after 1967. As an attorney, she has represented a number of Palestinian prisoners. She was very controversial in Israel, not least because of her campaign to highlight the torture and abuse of prisoners in Israeli prisons. She has also written books criticizing the system, some of which have been translated into English.

4 Some of these short prose pieces have been published in French in French journals. Many have also been translated into English, but have not yet been published.

9

I want to be free

Ghassan Zaqtan

Ghassan Zaqtan is presented in anthologies and periodicals as a new, fresh, modern voice. In the introduction to the translations of his poems in the *Anthology of Modern Palestinian Literature*, published in 1992, it says: "Zaqtan has clearly transcended his immediate predecessors who led the course of modern Arabic poetry since the early fifties. He belongs to that group of young Arab poets (among whom there are many Palestinians) who show the authentic marks of a modernist outlook and technique."

October 2003. I have been trying to get in touch with Ghassan Zaqtan for days, but he's not answering the phone. So I call my middleman Mahmoud Shuqair, to see if he knows anything, and he says that Zaqtan might be abroad. I feel the panic rising. Not him too! I haven't been able to get in touch with Mahmoud Darwish either. Each time I phone the Sakakini Cultural Center in Ramallah, where Darwish has his office, a woman tells me that Darwish is abroad and not likely to return within the year. Not only that, I keep trying to call the novelist and feminist Sahar Khalifeh on the numbers I've been given, and she's not answering either. For several hectic autumn days, it looks as though my project might fall apart.

Shuqair gives me an email address for Zaqtan and I send a desperate plea out into the night from an internet café on Jaffa Street, giving him the telephone number of the hotel where I'm staying in the old part of Jerusalem. When I get back to my room, the phone rings. It is Zaqtan. "Runo, I've heard about you and I've been waiting for you to get in touch. When are you coming to Ramallah? Tomorrow morning, early?"

So early the next morning I get into a sherut taxi, which fills up quickly, down by Damascus Gate. The drive to Ramallah is almost routine now. At the Kalandia checkpoint, you get out of the taxi and file past the Israeli soldiers—without much drama these days—and then get into another taxi on the other side for the last leg into the center of Ramallah. Jerusalem and Ramallah are so close that the journey really shouldn't take more than quarter of an hour. But in fact, with all the Israeli checkpoints, it takes a lot longer.

Early in the morning, going *to* Ramallah is relatively easy. *From* Ramallah back to Jerusalem is another story. At Kalandia, there are two lines leading up to the guards, and they are both long and fairly static. I practice my skills in interpreting facial expressions. The Israeli soldiers—young men and women, some of whom can be no older than eighteen—saunter back and forth, cigarettes dangling from the corners of their mouths, as if they had all the time in the world. The Palestinians both behind and in front of me in the line, young and old, men and women, are completely calm. Every now and then one of the soldiers up at the front barks at the line (which is perhaps thirty meters long) to move back five meters. The Palestinians then shuffle carefully back three steps only to go two forward again. As if they were in fact the constant, slow ebb and flow of the tide. Even when a soldier shouts and raises a gun to his shoulder, the Palestinians remain patient, standing with expressionless faces. I stand there trembling, more than ready to throw myself down in the dust.

I stand in the line and watch some enormous trucks leaving Ramallah; they have been stopped and the drivers ordered to lay their freight out on the road. I have no idea what the Israeli soldiers are saying to each other, but they appear to be joking around. One day I stood in one of these lines for over an hour, and the truck driver still hadn't finished getting everything out, he had so much. Boxes and boxes of diapers and shampoo were spread out on the road.

Every now and then a woman—and it is always a woman, never a man—explodes and starts to curse in the faces of these young soldiers. In the line behind her the men say nothing, but many of the women scream out what I can only assume is support.

Ghassan Zaqtan is sitting waiting for me when I bound up the steps and into his regular haunt, Zeryab, the artists' café in the center of Ramallah. He is an outgoing and youthful man with a bright smile. I immediately have to promise to come back the next day so he can drive me around Ramallah. He wants to show me all the beautiful places.

The waiter comes over. Zaqtan asks if I'm hungry. I shake my head, so we order coffee. I want to talk about Arabic and Palestinian modernism, because it obviously exists, only the world has not yet discovered it. So I start by referring to something that Zaqtan wrote back in 1988, which was almost a kind of manifesto, a plea for "a new corner from which to look" and at the same time a willingness "to destroy heroism as one destroys a rotten egg, together with valor, sorrow, love, chivalry, and all the other dinosaurs."[1] I ask him whether this was a conscious attempt to break with the past.

"Yes. My generation, those of us who started to write around 1980, started at a time when writing had in a way been ravaged by Palestinian politics for the past 40 to 50 years. Politics used literature for its own interests."

"As part of the fight for freedom?"

"Yes, it was quite normal at the time. And it's not that unusual these days either. But I decided right from the start that I would not be a leader. I would not head any demonstrations, I would not stand in the vanguard, on behalf of the people. That wasn't my duty as a writer. So I chose another position. If, for example, you're at the *back* of the demonstration, you might see some interesting things: a handkerchief, a shoe. You can see reality from many different angles. As a writer, you have to offer the reader new knowledge. But the most important thing is yourself, your memories, your way of seeing the world—colors, shadows, whatever. Everyone in my generation tried to free themselves from politics and the conflict. Personally, I have never seen my writing as part of the Israeli–Palestinian conflict, nor as a commentary on it. I like the Arabic language, which is incredibly flexible, and I like poetry—it helps me create a balance between myself and this difficult life. But of course, I live in Ramallah, and I *am* part of the conflict—but in my own way."

"How does the military occupation affect you, as a writer?"

Zaqtan shrugs and lights a cigarette. "This is our life. The occupation is our day-to-day reality, our everyday news. It's nothing new, not a shock or anything like that, it's a series of facts and knowledge. Palestinian culture faced its greatest challenge just after the Oslo Accords were signed, and the question was: what do we write about now? If your writing is a part of politics, then that is a legitimate question. But if instead you have chosen yourself to be the topic of your writing, you will generate new questions. So I write about my life. I don't try force myself *not* to write about the occupation, but if I do write about it, then it is based on *my own* experience, as an individual, confronting checkpoints and Israeli soldiers, or having to stay indoors for twenty days because there's a curfew. We live in an extremely difficult situation, but if you think of it as a source of inspiration for writing, then you can do something. That's what I am trying to do, to tell my own story."

He bursts out laughing, stubs out his cigarette in the ashtray. "The Israelis constantly give you new things to do, to write about, so it's entirely up to you. Sometimes our applications to travel to cultural events abroad are rejected. In the past year alone, I have had three applications turned down—one was for the Kapittel Festival of Literature and Freedom of Speech in Stavanger. And sometimes we are allowed to travel, of course, but it all depends on their mood. Every Palestinian has his or her own experience, and some of us have been held in Israeli prisons too."

The day after the interview, Zaqtan takes me on a little sightseeing trip in and around the town. At one point, we stand on a hill with an amazing view over the long valleys bathed in a golden autumn sun, and he tells me about the invasion last spring. At the time I was traveling in Israel, while the tanks were destroying the streets of Ramallah. The apartment block where Zaqtan lives was taken over as a base for a unit of soldiers. So all the families living there—over twenty people—were herded down into the cellar, forced into a small apartment, and put under curfew. There was, of course, not enough food or space, but Zaqtan says that the worst thing was having to put on a show for the children 24/7, to give the impression that everything was OK and that nothing bad would happen. That—Zaqtan tells me, gazing at the landscape that he loves so much—was terrible.

Partners

My meetings with Zaqtan provide many interesting opportunities to talk about the similarities and parallels between Palestine and the Palestinians on the one hand, and Israel and the Israelis on the other. And also to talk about some form of cultural exchange.

When I met Zaqtan, I already knew that he had some Israeli friends who were writers, including Etgar Keret, whose greetings I had promised to convey. Mentioning Izzat Ghazzawi's theory that there were no shared myths between Israelis and Palestinians, I asked him if he thought that literature could play a role in attempts to understand the other.

"I think that we, the Jews and the Palestinians, were cultural partners until Israel was established in 1948. I personally love music and I recently found out that my favorite singer, Laila Morad from Egypt, is Jewish. One of my favorite poets from classical Arabic literature is also a Jew. I think that it's a great mistake to equate Jewish and Israeli culture. I acknowledge the depth of Jewish culture, but Israeli culture is completely different. Most of my friends in Israel don't like to talk about it, but for me it is a fact."

"Are you referring to the difference between the Sephardic and Ashkenazi Jews?"

"Yes. I think that the minority in Israel has led the majority. The fact is that Arabs account for 20 percent of the population in Israel and Oriental Jews for 55 percent. So, 75 percent share the same culture, the same memories, and, to be blunt, belong here.

Then there is the 25 percent that is European, and the truth is that Israel wants to be Little Europe in the Middle East, which is impossible. If you want to be European, go to Europe."

"What about the Sephardic Jews today, do they also want to be part of Europe?"

"There's been a kind of masking, an attempt to change their memories. I know that the Holocaust was terrible and I can in no way ignore all that the Jews went through in Europe. At the same time, they are not Palestinian memories, nor are they Mizrahi memories. But in Israel, the Sephardic Jews have to adopt the memories of Ashkenazi Jews. These memories have been planted in their lives at the expense of their own. The Sephardic culture has been hijacked and that's not fair."

"Surely there has been a kind of leveling between the Sephardic and Ashkenazi Jews in Israel?"

"The Sephardic Jews were given an opportunity to exert their influence when the PLO returned in 1994, because they know our culture. I believe that peace, *real* peace, not Sharon's peace or Barak's—will give Israel a completely new chance, by toning down its European heritage and instead having it become a part of the Middle East. That's my opinion. Because the Jews were in fact our partners here. You could say that we shared a life and culture until 1948."

And today? Daily life is dominated by conflict and occupation. And while it is blindingly obvious that this does something to people, I still venture to ask if there is any point of contact between Israel and Palestine. Is there any form of cultural exchange?

Ghassan Zaqtan focuses on identity and says that it is a pressing issue for both the Palestinians and the Israelis.

"Culturally, the Palestinians are of course a part of the Arab world, but we are also unique because of this conflict. And we certainly have problems with our identity. Identity is a real issue here, more so than in any other Arab country. In that sense, we're like the Jews. But I want to point out that this hard and complex conflict has given the Palestinians something else as well. It's a bit like going somewhere new. You can't leave somewhere without taking something with you, and you can't be somewhere without giving something to it. It's impossible. You will always be a different person after leaving a place. I believe that the enemy is just like a place. That is, the 'enemy' in quotation marks. There is no conflict in which you don't take something from your 'enemy.' Ever."

"So, you have taken something from the Jewish heritage and/or mentality?"

"Yes."

"What's that?"

Zaqtan lights another cigarette, calls the waiter over and asks him to turn down the music, before clearing his throat. "We are their mirror image. You will find us in their writing. We are the flipside of their dreams, their lives. We can't be avoided. They can't ignore us, even though some of them try. When they go to extremes in order to ignore us, we just become more powerful in their minds. And the same is true for us. I personally have no problems acknowledging the influence that Israeli thought and culture have had on me."

He bursts out laughing and shrugs: "I see Israelis in my worst nightmares."

"You've read Keret, of course?"

"I've read his work in both English and Arabic, and I really like it. I've met quite a few Israeli authors at various international festivals and conferences. I actually stayed with Keret for three months, in the US.[2] We had long, long discussions and became good friends, but still disagree about a lot of things. His humane ideals are very close to my own. We really are partners in this conflict. We were both born into it, and this is our shared place, with only one hour between him in Tel Aviv and me in Ramallah. But when we talk about our memories, he talks about his grandfather in Europe."

"Does he talk about Poland?"

"Yes. That is his history, not mine. On the other hand, there is an elderly Iraqi Jew called Naïm Kattan, who lives in Canada. He has written a novel called *Farewell, Babylon,*[3] where he writes about life in Baghdad in the period around 1950. I love that book, the music, the sounds, everything. I don't agree with all his ideas, but

I feel very close to him. But in terms of what's happening here and now, we are miles apart. I also feel very close to Ronny Someck,[4] another Jewish writer who was born in Iraq and who now lives in Israel. It's all very complicated."

"You say that there are in fact stories of cooperation and understanding between Jews and Palestinians, from the period before 1948?"

"Yes, it's true. In Israel, they tried to invent a kind of Oriental holocaust for the Sephardic Jews, without much success."

"Is it possible that contemporary literature could reach back into these shared memories?"

"Well, we have now had 50 years of fighting, blood, and suffering, so it's no longer easy to talk about things like that."

"In which case, you would have to write historical fiction?"

"Yes. The most important thing is that they have to be honest about their memories, and we have to be honest about ours. Some Oriental Jews in Israel, for example Sami Michael [see chapter 7, note 2], have written largely in Arabic. On the other hand, you have Anton Shammas [see chapter 1, note 10], a Palestinian who was born and raised in Israel, who is not afraid to write in Hebrew. I know that a lot of people in various Arab countries have criticized Shammas for doing this, but I think he did a very good job. I don't know Yoram Kaniuk personally, but I like what he said: 'Shammas and I share the same nationality.' These people are trying to find solutions. I think that some of them—not all—are courageous. They say what they think. But all Israelis see Palestinian culture as the indigenous culture, not as something that is a part of their own movement. That is their greatest weakness."

Exile

I try to keep the focus on cultural exchange and ask if there are any concrete examples of what has migrated from Israel to the Palestinian territories and vice versa.

Ghassan Zaqtan mentions exile. The Israeli Jews talk about the 2,000 years of Diaspora, before their return to Israel. A life in exile and the journey back to Palestine/Israel is a well-trodden path in Hebrew literature.

And what does exile mean to the Palestinians? Most of today's leading writers in Palestine have lived in exile. They know Jordan, Lebanon, and Tunisia. They returned in 1994, in the wake of Arafat, the PLO, and the Palestinian National Authority.

I discuss with Zaqtan what a life in exile actually means and I ask what was it like to come back in 1994; I also ask about the relationship between the so-called returnees, those who came back after the Oslo Accords, and the Palestinians—writers included— who stayed in Palestine.

"That is a key question for us. Those of us who returned had our own experiences in exile, really positive experiences. We had been in contact with the cultural movements and literature of the Arab countries, of Europe and the rest of the world. Being in exile offered many opportunities, many more than we have here. But we didn't have a realistic image of this place, compared with those who had always lived here. We were more experimental, more language and style oriented, because we had lived in open societies. Those who stayed here have a far deeper and more direct understanding; they know this place in a completely different way from us, and they know the enemy better too. But to go back to what we were talking about. Cultural exchange. I think that we have taken a lot from the Jewish heritage, such as exile and the concept of the 'promised land.' You know, sometimes victims fall in love with their murderers. That's not quite what has happened here, but something similar. For the Palestinians in exile, Palestine became the promised land and we rebuilt it, mentally."

"But that was Haifa and Jaffa, wasn't it, not towns like Ramallah?"

"Oh yes, everything, the whole of ancient Palestine. In exile, all our suffering fueled our dreams. So when we came back here in 1994, we thought that this was paradise and we were totally shocked. This is a poor country with great suffering. Something else we have adopted from the Jews is the idea of a chosen people. We have always thought that we were the chosen ones, the guardians of the promised land. We embedded this in our culture and used it in different ways. Another similarity is the ghetto. If you go to Jordan or Lebanon, you will find huge refugee camps, a kind of Palestinian replica of the ghettos. They weren't intended to last for more than a year or two—they've been there for almost half a century now. There are Palestinian communities everywhere, even in Arab countries. In Spain, there are Palestinian writers who write in Spanish, and in the US and the UK, Palestinians write in English or Arabic. We're now trying to get to know this incredibly diverse and rich culture of ours. After 1994, we had the opportunity to gather all this together, but we didn't. Primarily because the Palestinian National Authority had no experience governing people. Even though I myself am in a way part of the authorities, I can honestly say that they made a big mistake. They came from outside, took up their positions and started to govern, without any dialogue—not even with the intelligentsia. Today there is a very real gap between the authorities and the people."

The Writer's Responsibility

Ten years have now passed since Arafat and the Palestinian leaders returned, followed by a succession of writers, including Zaqtan. I ask what Zaqtan sees as the position and role of writers in Palestine today. Does he feel that they are respected and listened to? And what about the position of literature?

"*Yanni*, I feel like starting all my answers with 'maybe, I'm not sure.' The current situation is very difficult for us writers. One consequence of Israel's invasions in recent years is that the Palestinian middle class has been more or less eradicated. We first lost our middle class in spring 1948, when our towns and the coast were taken over, and now it's happening again. By middle class I mean people who can generate, express, and write about opinions. Israel has succeeded in that sense: many Palestinian writers and intellectuals have moved abroad. I have tried to buy new books, but there hasn't been a single new book here in Ramallah in the past two years. You can only get the few that are actually published here in Ramallah, all other books are banned. Personally, this is less of a problem for me, as I travel abroad a fair amount, but what about the students? There has been no real dialogue with Israeli culture in the past three years, or with Arab culture. The only Israelis we can talk to are the soldiers, and they are everywhere. It's difficult to get anything to grow in this climate, difficult to find out anything about the world. My last book, for example, was published in Lebanon and Jordan and now, a good year after publication, it has still not reached Ramallah."

André Brink's positive experience from South Africa is something I share with all the Israeli and Palestinian authors that I meet. This is clearly a question with no set answer, so in reality, it's a matter of what each author believes is possible, or can imagine. What about Zaqtan, can he imagine the situation in Palestine changing as it did in South Africa?

"It's too early to say. The conflict is extremely fierce."

"It was fierce in South Africa too."

"Yes, but the situation is more complex here. In South Africa, the blacks could go to Johannesburg and the whites could go to the black villages. I can't even go directly to our own university, Birzeit. There are 420 Israeli checkpoints in the West Bank, that tiny scrap of land. They have destroyed everything and won't let people go to work. In South Africa, the whites used the blacks for labor, and in that way kept them alive, but we don't even have *that* here. There are about 300,000 workers without jobs, and no books are allowed in. It is desperately hard, far worse than you can imagine. But we do have one vital thing, the internet. The internet is used more here than in any other Arab country, basically because we need it. It's the only means we have to avoid isolation. You've probably noticed that there are plenty of internet cafés here in Ramallah. Availability is obviously not so good in many other towns, not to mention villages. As a result of the situation here, an incredible network of paths has been created between towns and villages, which people use to avoid the checkpoints. There are even guides, and maps have that been carved onto trees. It's incredible what people will do when forced to, because they have to get to university or the clinic. But it's not normal, at all. What will our children be like after three years of such violence? As Palestinians, we have to think about the next generation. We may not see the consequences today, but in ten years perhaps they will appear. We need to develop a national strategy, or there will be a high price to pay."

Faced with such a reality, what, if anything, does Zaqtan think that writers can offer?

Like all the other Palestinian authors, Zaqtan mentions the case of the Israeli pilots who refused to bomb civilian targets in the Palestinian territories. Israeli authors then came out in support of these pilots. This can only be a positive thing, right?

"Yes, I was very glad to see that some Israeli writers and artists signed the petition. Very positive. And during the olive harvest last year, Amos Oz and some other Israeli authors gave their support to Palestinian farmers. That makes me feel good. But unfortunately that's not always the case. I think that the Israeli intelligentsia has to do more—not in Palestine, but in Israel. They have to tell their people and leaders that they don't accept what they are doing in the Palestinian territories."

"One problem is perhaps that they don't know what is actually going on in Palestine?"

"Most people don't want to know. It's easier for them to just ignore it. If they admit that they know, then they have to assume greater responsibility. And I don't think that they're ready to do that, but they *must*. It's impossible to escape reality. Not everyone was in favor when the Oslo Accords were signed, but we were the ones who had to pay the price, while Israel got off free. And Israeli writers have a responsibility in that context. During the war in Lebanon in 1982, Israeli writers and intellectuals mobilized enormous demonstrations and really helped change opinion. This touched us deeply, and shocked us, because we weren't aware of this internal opposition. But declamations aren't enough anymore, we need a grassroots movement. But perhaps they're frightened. Perhaps they like their cultural ghetto."

"I've met a number of Israeli intellectuals who would like to hear *your* voices when it comes to the suicide bombers. What do you say to that?"

"We are against it, and we *have* protested. Over a thousand Palestinian writers and intellectuals signed a petition last summer that appeared in our papers for three months. And we certainly paid for it. You know this place, so you can imagine how difficult it was for us."

Fear and Freedom

The freedom of writers is something I discuss with all the Palestinian writers I interview, on the understanding that it is a question with no clear answer. There are no rules that unequivocally state: "Do not write about the following topics." It is more a question of what each individual feels are the limits of his freedom.

"Do you mean in relation to the authorities or society?"

"Both, I guess."

"Sometimes I get anxious and frightened. But I stand for what I write. I have a regular weekly column in the *Al-Ayyam* paper and yesterday I wrote openly about the two latest suicide bombs. And yes, I got some phone calls. I have spoken out against the Palestinian Authority too, against the mentality of the secret service and against Arafat himself. In a way we are totally free here, not because we have a proper democracy, but because the authorities are so weak. And because the conflict has been going on for so long, new traditions have also evolved. For example, we're probably the only place in the Arab world to have around fourteen local TV channels. They're all completely independent, popular, and weak. We also have around twenty radio stations, where you can really talk about whatever you want. It's important that we protect what we have now, otherwise it won't be easy to carry on later."

In addition to his writing, Zaqtan has a permanent job as a journalist and editor for a periodical. He has previously worked for the Ministry of Culture, as have Mahmoud Shuqair and other authors. I question this close connection with the authorities and ask him if he finds it a problem.

"In Israel, they call different generations of Hebrew authors different names, so I would say that I belong to the PLO generation. My generation was born into the PLO. Our country was the PLO. Before 1994, most people saw us as fighters. Then 1994 happened and the PLO returned to Palestine, and what did we do? Well, writers just continued in the same tradition without reflecting the change in conditions: that we were now in Palestine, the true homeland, not the land of the PLO. The Ministry of Culture is a disaster and has fallen to pieces because it never managed to establish political goals. So most writers have left."

"Does it also have something to do with the fact that power corrupts?"

"Yes. Most writers quit the Ministry because we started to ask ourselves similar questions after several years. I don't want to be part of it, I want to be free, I'm a writer. But most of us are still supported by the authorities and the PLO."

"Financially?"

"Yes. But the reality is that the Palestinian intelligentsia's influence on politics waned after 1982, when the PLO pulled out of Beirut. Politicians hijacked all policy until 1994. There was in fact no dialogue before the Oslo Accords, there was no intellectual movement that fought for its ideas. It's only now, during the second intifada, that we have finally started to hear voices again, here and there. Edward Said[5] came a few times, and he wrote extensively and with great courage. He also spoke out against the Oslo Accords. And then there's Darwish, who resigned from the PLO because of the Oslo Accords.[6] He was asked to be minister of culture three times, but refused each time. However, he has chosen to stay here in Ramallah. These two, and Emile Habibi before he died, have forced the Palestinian intelligentsia to think. But our institutions are in ruins. The Writers' Union no longer functions. The Ministry of Culture does nothing. I mean that and I've written about it too. But culture still survives, here and there, in places like the Sakakini Cultural Center. I think that centers like that are the best way to kick-start our cultural growth again."

Modernism

I have read some of Ghassan Zaqtan's poetry, and the first thing that struck me was his sparkling and inventive imagery and the focus on sensuality and death.

In some of his finest poems, these two themes play off each other. For example, in *Secret Connections*: "We should swim together in the stream / and lie down like two wet sponges on the banks, / while the water runs from our clothes / we should let the silence hide us, / feel the peace and listen without a sound / till we can see each other's breath." The poem describes a meeting between two people, who might even be children, and there is something beautiful, but secret, even forbidden, about it. And then, in the final line, this atmosphere is punctured: "We forget that they have sent a little one to Khirba where the little ones / are laid in the ground."[7]

Death is never far away. You can, like the young people by the stream, keep death at a distance for a while, but only for a while.

If death is the main character in Zaqtan's poetic universe, then sensuality plays the next most important role. And when I say sensuality, I mean the way in which the eyes see in these poems. A love of life, desire. With Zaqtan, desire and light often spill over into something else: "Your open blouse comes toward me / releasing a scream within my breast / a terrible fear, a wound."

His poems are about desire and death as universal values, and how the two seem to be intertwined. Could his poems be described as unmistakably Palestinian? No, not really. I ask Zaqtan whether he thinks there is something unique about Palestinian storytelling.

"No, I don't think so. We're really part of the Arab heritage and Arab culture. We share the same masters, the same history, the same themes and questions."

He frowns, and thinks for a while. There is a small mountain of cigarette butts in the ashtray between us; this interview has taken some time.

"Well, perhaps we do have something peculiar to us, because of the conflict. So there is a difference, a difference of degree. We have our own questions and problems when it comes to identity. You've met Salman Natour [see chapter 15], haven't you? He's a Palestinian, an Israeli, an Arab…"

"Yes, when I met Salman Natour, this was how he put it: 'Personally, I don't need a Palestinian identity. For me, it's enough to be Arab. But because of the political conflict here, I say that I'm a Palestinian. It's political, not cultural.' Would you agree?"

"Yes, I agree. But at the same time, writers such as Salman Natour and Anton Shammas are also part of *Israeli* culture."

"One final question. Based on everything you've talked about, would you say that the Palestinian identity is connected to exile, a series of tragedies, being a victim?"

Zaqtan smiles and holds out his hands: "The Palestinian identity is a mixture of all that, and more."

NOTES

1 These quotations are from Salma Khadra Jayyusi's foreword to *Anthology of Modern Palestinian Literature* (New York: Columbia University Press, 1992). She credits them to Ghassan Zaqtan, "First Words Are Fascinating and We Shall Remember Them," *Al-Filer al-dimograti* 3 (Summer 1998): 192–193.

2 Both Keret and Zaqtan participated in the International Writing Program at the University of Iowa.

3 *Adieu, Babylone* (Montréal: La Presse, 1975). Published the following year in France (Paris: Juillard, 1976). Later also translated into English by Sheila Fischman and published in the US as *Farewell, Babylon* (New York: Taplinger, 1980).

4 The poet Ronny Someck was born in Baghdad in 1951 and moved to Israel as a boy. A collection of his poems has been published in English, German, French, Albanian, and Arabic.

5 Edward Said (1935–2003) was born in Jerusalem to Palestinian parents. He grew up in Egypt and later in the US, where he studied comparative literature and was awarded a professorship at Columbia University. He wrote many books, of which *Orientalism* (1978) is perhaps the best known. It has been translated into many languages. He also wrote books and articles about the conflict in the Middle East and was generally regarded as the international voice of the Palestinians. When I was in Ramallah in autumn 2003, there were posters of him on all the walls and houses, in commemoration and as a mark of respect.

6 For more about Darwish's reasons, see Mona Naim (1995).

7 This poem is not available in English translation and has been translated from the Norwegian. *Trans.*

10

My aim is to survive

Liana Badr

Liana Badr has worked on women's rights and related issues for many years, and her books focus on women. Therefore I was interested to hear what she had to say about the position of women in Palestine and Palestinian literature today. Her literary work is also rooted in Palestinian history as a series of losses, not least *al-Nakba* ("the catastrophe") in 1948, when around 750,000 Palestinians were driven from the newly established state of Israel; then the Six-Day War in 1967, which resulted in Israel's occupation of the West Bank and Gaza and, for many, a life in exile thereafter. How does a female writer tackle these subjects?

Liana Badr and I had been corresponding by email for some time before I went to Israel in April 2002, and she was very keen to meet me. While I was there, I stayed for a few days at a convent by the Sea of Galilee, as I waited for the Israeli forces to withdraw from the West Bank so that I could get in. I rang Badr from this idyll. She was apoplectic. She raged against Israel and the new occupation and railed against the Jewish settlements on the hills above Ramallah. Much of the shooting was coming from there. Her office window faced that direction and she no longer dared use the office for fear of getting shot, so she had to make do with her small kitchen. I mentioned the Portuguese writer and Nobel laureate José Saramago, who had recently visited the area and had angered Israelis—writers and others—by drawing a parallel between Ramallah and Auschwitz. "That's absolutely true!" Badr thundered into the receiver. I recall I was quiet for a moment as I searched for something suitable to say. And I remember thinking to myself that even though we were so close now, she in Ramallah and me at the beautiful Tabgha by the Sea of Galilee, I was still unable to see and truly understand what she was going through.

That was in spring 2002, and I finally met her in autumn 2003. "Just come," she assured me when I called. "I'll be waiting in my office at the Ministry of Culture."

Once in the center of Ramallah, I ask the first person I meet for directions. The last time I was in the area, battles raged in these streets with not a person to be seen, only Israeli tanks. Now it's like any other town, with people coming and going and no stress. They are polite and welcoming.

I can only see one building in the vicinity that matches the description I was given, but can that dirty, gray, shabby building really be the Ministry of Culture?

It is and soon I'm sitting in Liana Badr's bare office. On the way in, she points to a message she has written on the white wall: "To all Israeli soldiers. This is the Ministry of Culture. We work with culture here—literature, film, art, and theater."

"Not that I think it helps, you can but hope. During the occupation last year, they took over the whole place and used it as a base. It's a tall building in a strategic position. Come over here and look out the back. A view straight to Mukata, where Arafat stays. So the Israeli soldiers lived in these corridors and offices for months and months. It was in a terrible state when we were finally allowed back in. They had broken everything. PCs and other equipment had been thrown against the walls. As you can see, I still haven't gotten a new computer, and I'm the Palestinian Ministry of Culture's director of art! I was one of the first people to come here once the soldiers had left. I took a video camera and film with me to document it. You wouldn't believe it. They had urinated and defecated everywhere and the smell was disgusting. Beyond description. I've finished editing the film now, so you will see it tomorrow.[1] It took us weeks and weeks to get all the muck out, wash the place, and start to settle back in. That's the way things are here. It's not the first time that they have occupied this building, and I'm afraid it won't be the last, either."

Liana Badr is a passionate woman with a lot on her mind. So much, in fact, that our interview is spread over three mornings. As her writing is so closely linked to her own life, it seems only right to start with a brief biography.

Badr was born in Jerusalem in 1952 and grew up in Jericho, where her father had a medical practice. During the Six-Day War in 1967, she fled with her father and four younger siblings to Amman. They were refugees and had lost their house and belongings. Badr soon became involved with the resistance and married another known activist, Yasser Abed Rabbo, who later served as a minister under Arafat for many years.

Following Black September (1970),[2] she ended up in Beirut, where she worked as a journalist and a volunteer in the Palestinian refugee camps in Sabra and Shatila. She worked to improve the conditions for women in particular. She then had her own children and started to write. In 1982, when the Palestinians were forced out of Beirut, she went to Damascus in Syria.

"Once again, I lost everything I owned, but I kept on writing in Damascus. I interviewed a number of Palestinian refugees because I wanted to rebuild what had been destroyed. I realized that the Israelis would continue to persecute us and try to obliterate our memories, so I thought I could do the opposite, I could save lives—by remembering."

Following disputes between the PLO and the Syrian authorities, Badr moved again in 1987, this time to Tunis. And she kept on writing. She felt very strongly that she was working on a special project.

"A historical project. I wanted to write about the history of Palestine from a woman's point of view. Women barely featured in Palestinian literature before then. And if they did, it was as secretaries, mothers, and sisters, but never as people."

Thus a framework of themes became clear: the project was about remembering and documenting reality through the medium of literature. Her work deals with the Palestinian catastrophes, life in exile, the role and struggles of women. In both her novels and short stories, the action in the present often takes place in exile in Lebanon, with subplots leading back to the characters' experiences in the past.

A Balcony over the Fakihani comprises three novellas set in present-day Lebanon, with retrospective action. "The Canary and the Sea" is about Abu Husain, a refugee from 1948. In 1982, the Israelis invade and take over Beirut airport. Abu Husain and his patrol stumble on an Israeli position and come under fire. The other Palestinians are killed, and Abu Husain is badly injured. He lies on the ground and begs the Israeli soldiers to help him.

When I discuss this story with Liana Badr, I comment on the Jewish characters, or more accurately, the soldiers.

"It's a true story. Abu Husain was a real person, I talked to him after this happened. I think that of all my stories, this one is the closest to a documentary. Every single detail is true."

"So Abu Husain was wounded and asked the soldiers for help, but they wanted money. Isn't that a bit of a cliché, the Jew who always thinks about money?"

"No, no, no. Everything in that novella is true. I've always worked in the opposite way from García Márquez and other Latin American writers, who use their imagination to create literature. I always say that we need to take the imagination out of our lives in order to create literature. My literary work has always been like that. I don't add things, I strip them away. Because if you were to give a literary portrayal of Palestinian lives, it would soon start to sound like magical realism."

Equal Conditions

In Badr's books, the Jew is always a soldier. But why is that? I ask her if there are no other images or experiences.

"If you don't want to listen to the other side's stories, then you will never solve any problems. The Palestinians have tried to listen. They have worked in Israel, and have their own memories from before 1948, which are interlinked with the Jews'. My husband's family, for example, were from Jaffa and his mother only wore clothes from Jewish shops. His father was a fruit seller and had many contacts and friends in the Jewish community. And who were the Jews who were living here then? The Sephardic Jews, of course, descendants of the Spanish Jews who were banished from Spain in 1492, along with the Arabs. So if you look back to our roots, you will find that the Sephardic Jews and the Palestinians have a shared experience. We were both banished from Spain. We accepted them. But then they suddenly got this idea that they're better than other people, that they are chosen by God… And that has led to increasing fanaticism on our part too. If fanatics accounted for only one percent before, they now account for around five percent."

On the third and final day that I meet Badr, I point out an apparent contradiction in her account. On the one hand, she claims that the Palestinians understand the Israeli Jews (whereas the Jews do not understand the Palestinians), not least because they have worked for Israelis in Israel. On the other hand, she admits that the portrayal of the Jew in Palestinian literature is largely limited to one stereotype, the soldier.

"Take me, for example, or any of the other Palestinians who came back here after the Oslo Accords—we haven't lived or worked in Israel, so for us, the Israeli *is* a soldier. The same applies to small children, to me, to everyone. It was true in Lebanon and it's true in Palestine today. Coming back was a shock. As Palestinians living in exile, we had experienced a wealth of impulses, but here there were no bookstores, no books—nothing. My own family didn't even know what I wrote about. They knew I was well known, but they had never read my work because they couldn't get hold of my books. So I have gradually worked my way up again since I came back."

Liana Badr talks in a steady stream, the words pour out, and she barely pauses for breath. Managing to slip in a follow-up question requires determination and timing. There is a knock at the door, and an elderly gentleman comes in with two cups on a tray, coffee for me and tea for the director. The man backs out of the room, then the phone rings. Badr is just as intense in her telephone conversations as she is with me, and the second she puts down the receiver, she continues with her exegesis.

"Don't get me wrong, I know some good, peace-loving Israelis, but the vast majority of Israelis that I meet are soldiers. The Palestinians who have always lived here know the Israelis as masters and bosses as well, but that's not an equal relationship either. They knew what Israelis did and thought, but they were not able to love them, simply because the relationship was not equal. The Palestinian was the worker, the one who did all the dirty work. He didn't go out to Israeli restaurants and enjoy himself."

I mention Ghazzawi's theory about the lack of shared stories or myths and am interested to hear what Badr has to say about it.

"Our approach is completely different. The starting point for Palestinians is a multicultural existence, not a single national state or one religion. Palestine was a place for all people, races, and religions, especially the towns. I myself was brought up in a Muslim environment and my parents were at times non-believing communists. We also lived among Christians. My identity is multicultural. I feel that I carry with me a heritage from all races and all religions. In terms of history, I am connected to all the epochs in this area and all the people who have lived here. In my memories there is an equal relationship. I used to go to church on Christmas Eve in Jericho with my Christian friends, something that I write about in my novel *A Compass for the Sunflower*. And my Christian friends joined us for our Muslim celebrations. That was quite usual in Palestine at the time. That is our heritage and that heritage is also connected to the Jews who lived in Palestine."

The Jews are included up until 1948, and then there is a change.

"In other words, I grew up with three religions that respected each other. The Qur'an teaches respect for other people and religions. At the same time, it is very practical and pragmatic: Muhammad made contact with all kinds of people and showed them respect in order to strengthen his position. The opposite was true of the Jews, and when I say that, I mean Zionism, which is an egocentric movement. With Zionism came the desire to dominate and confiscate, and that's where the problem lies. When they established Israel, they had this concept of purity; they wanted an unblemished land only for the Jews. They were frightened of the world and wanted to be by themselves. Personally, I would never have been able to enjoy the world if I lived only with Muslims, because in Palestine, I lived with all kinds of nationalities and religions. For them, the opposite is true. They gather Jews from lots of different civilizations and unite them with this feeling of being Israeli. And that is not healthy. In this global age, people are less national and more cosmopolitan. I—and everyone around me—grew up with three religions that respected each other. So for me, the problem is not that they are Israeli, the problem is that they are occupiers."

Palestinian Women

As a writer and filmmaker, Liana Badr has focused on the position of women in Palestinian society, both in exile and in Palestine itself. So, sitting here in her office overlooking Ramallah, can she say that her work for women has borne fruit? Or are the classical gender roles still very much alive?

"They are very much alive, and they've gotten worse! Very few young Palestinian women today challenge the traditional gender roles. We are living under military siege and don't have much contact with the outside world, which results in a kind of mental siege as well. So now there's an almost tribal mentality here, which makes it extremely difficult for women, especially in the villages. The truth is that we live in a totally patriarchal society in Palestine. It will only be possible to change this if and when we manage to achieve a better life—and independence."

"Do you mean, for example, that women aren't free to choose their husbands, like Aisha in your novel *The Eye of the Mirror*?"[3]

"No, not that sort of thing. Women are perhaps freer than before to say yes or no. But if you're a married woman in Palestine, you have to accept everything. You have to work, be a servant. As a woman, you have no voice. I myself have periods when I find it extremely hard—I know I can get rid of the feeling, but I feel it all the same. When I get involved in something, the men look at me, as if to say, why have *you* come? Why are *you* here?"

"As a rule, you write about young girls. Aisha in *The Eye of the Mirror* isn't exactly a typical Palestinian protagonist."

"I chose a young girl because I wanted an anti-hero. Because Palestinian literature is full of male heroes, with a few exceptions, and they are very good and very generous, and they are always right, politically."

"Are you saying that Palestinian literature is generally political literature?"

"Well, the political literature is there, but I don't regard it as literature. I have always believed that literature should be judged on the basis of literary criteria. But if there's a political backdrop to a story, that's not a problem. My literary characters often talk about politics, particularly the older women, because that's what happens in reality. Just go into any Palestinian refugee camp—they discuss politics all day long."

"Is it possible to talk about Palestinian literature as a single entity? Is there, for example, a particularly Palestinian way of writing or telling stories?"

"No, but the same applies to literature the world over. There is no specific national voice. Personally, I try to cultivate polyphony in my literature."

The Roles of Literature

In Badr's view, Palestinian literature has played an important role over the years. And it has helped form a kind of national Palestinian identity.

"When you live with people who are weak, who are oppressed, occupied, controlled, imprisoned, humiliated, murdered, then as a writer, you are the voice of freedom that brings a sense of pride. Because literature is the bird of freedom in your soul. That is what we feel, literature gives us a sense of pride, it is somehow living out our humanity—despite the pressure from everything that is trying to destroy all that is human in us. So it gives us strength and it also opens the way for dialogue with others. I believe that literature is a very good means for the Palestinians to communicate with the rest of the world."

"Yes, let's talk a little about literature's potential role in the conflict. Do you think that it's possible to get to know and to understand more about the other side through literature?"

"Yes, a writer can learn a lot about the other side through literature. But I think we need a more holistic approach, where literature is an element of the process. Such a holistic approach would require a sound understanding of the other side, certainly a better one than we have today. And that means that the Israelis have to win over their fear of the Arabic language. Right now, the Palestinians are living behind physical walls, but the Israelis are living behind invisible walls. They know nothing about us, whereas you can read articles translated from Hebrew in our newspapers every day."

"Written by David Grossman, for example."

"Yes, but not just him. When I came back in 1994, I thought that literature would have a part to play. But then I discovered that even though I could read their literature—a lot of it has been translated into Arabic, and I can also read it in English—if you go to Israel, you won't find a single word of our literature translated into Hebrew. They know nothing about our cultural life. I once bumped into Amos Oz at an airport and I gave him *The Eye of the Mirror*. It was the start of a friendship. He even tried to get it translated into Hebrew, but nothing happened. The prevailing mood in Israel is to ignore the Palestinians."

"Darwish has recently been translated into Hebrew."

"Yes, but only him. He's a writer of international repute and his books have been translated into 30 languages. So perhaps a handful of peace activists in Israel had him translated."

Liana Badr hasn't written much since 1994. She has only published one book, a collection of poems written over the years.

She gets up, goes over to the window and points. "The whole of Ramallah is surrounded by Jewish settlements. You see the biggest of the hills over there? That is Pesagot. The people there start to shoot if they so much as hear a bird. I live nearby and lots of people in the neighborhood have been killed. So how can I talk about myself as an author? I don't feel that I am talking to you as an author, or a director, but rather as a *survivor*. My aim is to survive. I don't have goals anymore, as I did once, because I don't have the security, I feel that I can't control anything."

She sits down. The telephone rings again—it rings a lot—and she talks, listens, replies, then puts the phone down, looks at me and carries on talking. She has an impressive ability to pick up exactly where she left off.

"Before, when I was in exile, I lived in a big prison on the outside. Now I'm sitting in a small cage on the inside. I have family in Jerusalem, but I can't get there because the road is blocked. And as for writing, well, I've only published one collection of poetry in the past nine years. When I came back, I couldn't write anything because I didn't know anything about the homeland after 27 years in exile. I had to discover it, through my work here and the films that I made. I find no peace when I try to write. It's really difficult to concentrate when you're under an existential threat. Amos Oz said to me: 'You are a writer, you must continue to write. Life is so full.' But for me, there is nothing. Should I forever keep on sighing and complaining about what the Israelis are doing to me? That Israeli soldiers the same age as my sons snatch my ID papers from me, throw them on the ground and then laugh in my face? How can I write about my life? No one here has a life. There is no life in Palestine."

No Culture

And so, over the course of our three meetings, the conversation— or perhaps I should say monologue—veers from desperation to a faint glimmer of hope and then back to desperation. Liana Badr emphasizes the importance of her work at the Ministry of Culture.

"I feel that my work here is very important. That I'm helping to establish Palestinian culture. Culture can save us, and if you create a culture between people, then you can achieve peace—the two things are interconnected."

But creating Palestinian culture today is not a simple task.

"If you want to know what the role of the writer is today, there is only one answer: the writer has been marginalized. When we came back to Palestine in 1994, there was no culture here, so we established bookshops, printing works, cultural festivals, and more. The Ministry also opened 73 libraries, and with financial support from abroad, we now have ambitious plans for the distribution of children's literature. So we're trying, but we're constantly under threat. The Israelis have occupied and destroyed this building several times. And right now, nothing is happening, no projects, no grants, nothing. So how are people supposed to believe in culture?"

I ask her whether, as a writer, she finds working for Ministry of Culture a problem, and whether she feels that it compromises her independence.

Badr shakes her head resolutely. "The job is technical. I carry on with the technical work, and at the same time have the freedom to be myself. We're not really a national Palestinian authority because we have no state. So I'm working in a kind of transition phase, in order to create a state. When I came back in 1994, I really wanted to work for the Ministry of Culture, because then I would be working for the PLO, not a government. I have always believed that the PLO is the Palestinians' means to a political existence. It's a kind of revolutionary act, working for the people around you, without the benefits and privileges that are part and parcel of the private sector. And we're not well paid."

'All in all, do you feel that you are free as a Palestinian writer?'

"I'm free to write and have always written about what I want to write about, because I have my own style. I know how to write about things that it's not acceptable to write about, I have my own way. If people don't like what I write or think I'm too daring, that's their problem, not mine. I've been brought up to defend my freedom, so that's not the problem. We also have a publishing house here and I'm free to publish in any other Arab country, whenever I want. The problem is the occupation and the blockade that we have to live with, that is what limits our freedom. In a situation like this, writing becomes a luxury. Before, I vowed that I would write every day, but now I'm too frightened and anxious, and don't have the energy. With Israeli tanks thundering around me, writing is no longer foremost in my mind."

NOTES

1 *SIEGE: A Writer's Diary* is the name of the film, produced by the Creative Women's Forum, 2003.

2 The Palestinian Liberation Organization (PLO) was established in 1964 as an umbrella organization for various Palestinian opposition groups. Arafat became head of the organization in 1969. The PLO operated from Jordan in particular in its infancy, but then grew so strong that the Jordanian government felt threatened. In September 1970, the Jordanian army launched an attack on guerilla Palestinian forces, and all the guerillas were either killed or expelled in the course of spring 1971.

3 *The Eye of the Mirror* is Badr's best-known novel. It takes place in the Tal Ezza'Tar refugee camp between 1975 and 1976 and is based on true events. The camp was besieged by Lebanese Phalangists and the siege ended with the horrific massacre of the Palestinian refugees.

11

I write to release the violence inside

Zakariyya Muhammad

Zakariyya Muhammad is one of Palestine's most critically acclaimed poets and has also written novels and books about Palestinian culture and history. The introduction to *Anthology of Modern Palestinian Literature* says: "We have Zakariyya Muhammad (b. 1951), who, above all others, has more radically broken with the old heroic stance, the stance of the poet as hero and liberator shouldering great national responsibilities. Instead we find a new, ironic and self-critical poetry."

When I called Zakariyya Muhammad to see if we could meet, he was uncertain. He had not been well recently, he explained. But when I suggested an hour or so in a café, he thought that might be possible. The man who comes up the steps and into Café Zeryab in Ramallah one day in October 2003 is hesitant and careful. He slowly makes his way over between the tables. Even though I am obviously the only Westerner in the café, he doesn't come directly over. I get up and go to meet him.

Muhammad is first and foremost a poet, but he is also a painter and a sculptor. I have been looking forward to meeting him and to having the opportunity to discuss Palestinian modernism, as he very much spearheaded the movement. What is Palestinian modernism? We know that traditionally Arabic poetry has belonged to the people and has since time immemorial been sung and recited in Arab cafés and around tables. But what about today? Is the man on the street in Ramallah familiar with modernism?

Muhammad smiles gently, before complaining in a quiet voice that he has a sore back. He is a man who allows himself a moment to reflect before answering. I start by referring to the widespread perception that Palestinian literature and political activism are linked.

"You're not considered to be a political writer, are you?"

"No, I don't think so. I sometimes write newspaper articles, and then I am political. But in my poetry, I slam the door on politics and write about other things: life, death, or an ant, for that matter. But perhaps indirectly... I think that you can feel the *violence* in my words, in my metaphors. Sometimes I think I write to release the violence inside me."

This inner violence relates, of course, to the prevailing situation. So I ask him what it is like to be a writer in Palestine today.

"It's very difficult to be a writer here these days—if you want to be good. We are denied access to so much. We have no proper libraries, so doing research is hopeless. No proper cinemas or art exhibitions. No new books have been allowed in for a couple of years. And on top of that, we're locked into a situation where we're forced to be interested in politics, because politics is our life here. But I've always said, right from the start, that I would not let the occupation dictate the scope of my work. Because if all you write about is torture and checkpoints, it means the other side has won and is influencing your poetry. They can occupy my house, my street, my country, but I will not let them occupy my poems. I will write about what I want to write about. So I write as if I'm a poet anywhere else in the world, as if the occupying forces weren't on my back. Why should a Norwegian poet have the privilege of writing about a rose, when I have to be satisfied with tanks? So, I've kicked the tanks out of my poems. And yes, I do absolutely belong to the generation of poets that has abandoned politics."

"Along with names such as Ghassan Zaqtan?"

"Yes, and others. It all started around 1980. We were a small, isolated group back then. But now most Palestinian authors have moved away from politics. Maybe we have even gone toward the other extreme."

"You mean that you have become too private and inward-looking?"

"Yes, as a marked reaction to the earlier political poetry. I honestly don't know whether it's a good or a bad thing, this focus on the personal. I started to write novels as well. A novel can contain everything, so it's not such a problem to include social and political issues. My novels are more political, but only in a way that reflects daily life, and daily life *is* politics. Anyone coming to Ramallah from one of the villages has to deal with a series of political issues on the way, Israeli checkpoints being one of them."

"Could we just go back to modernist poetry and your suggestion that the modernist movement may come at a price?"

"Yes, poetry doesn't play the same role as it used to, which is also a result of the fact that people are financially and politically worn down. They're not looking for poetry; they're looking for ways to survive. But even if only a small minority buys books now, I would say that people still like poetry. Our poetry is not directly linked to national issues anymore, and it's more complex than before."

"So the reader needs to be fairly well educated?"

"Yes. I don't know whether it's a good thing or not, that the complexity can disrupt any direct communication between poetry and the reader. Sometimes I think it's good, that it's in the interest of poetry—poetry has to protect itself. To bow to the reader would ruin the poem. At other times I think no, some form of communication is needed. It's a difficult dilemma."

Muhammad believes that Mahmoud Darwish marks a clear change in Palestinian literature, which for a long time was marginal in an Arabic context. Following Darwish's debut in the 1960s, Palestinian literature has been at the center.

"Darwish has done an amazing job, and he still writes well today. But in a way, I and my generation rebelled against Darwish."

"Either you had to be as good as him, on his terms, or you had to come up with something completely different?"

"Exactly, and that's a form of influence as well. He forced me to go another way, to abandon his language and his way of doing things. So I'm a sort of inverse of Darwish. We have spurned politics, rejected epic poems, ignored his vocabulary and created our own dictionary."

And what does this new dictionary look like? The long poem "Apology,"[1] written in 1978, opens like this: "I was never a knight / nor a fruitful tree / I never gave to those who love me / any shade."

It is in every way an anti-heroic poem. The first-person narrator looks back over his life and sees his own fear, shame, and sorrow. And apologizes for his existence: "And apologizing for my life / authorizing my funeral to be at night / so that no-one attend it."

There is, however, something about the tone and choice of words that prevents the poem from spilling over into sentimentality. A particular kind of humor shines through at various points: "I hesitated when I invented my hand / I hesitated when I asked my questions / I hesitated when I thought / that hesitation was my pivot / and my virtue."

Universal qualities such as loneliness and tristesse run through his poems. Sometimes it's possible to discern specific Palestinian experiences coming to the surface, but the poems can easily be read on more than one level. They don't close, they open.

Bringing the focus back to the moment, I ask a more general question: "As a writer, what are you trying to achieve?"

"Well, I have a troubled relationship with poetry. I have never felt certain that poetry is effective, that it can achieve anything important. So I ask myself, what is poetry, why is there a need for it, what is its use? Maybe it would be better for me to grow tomatoes? I was constantly on the verge of abandoning poetry. My first collection was called *The Last Poems* [1981]. The second was more optimistic, *Handcraft* [1990]. I took my third title from a Turkish saying that is something like 'Things happen, there's nothing to be done about it' [1994]. That's a bit like my relationship to poetry. The fact that something has happened, something that I can't let go. I think that poetry achieves small things, but not great things. Like a hand mill, it only works slowly. Poetry does things slowly, but it goes deep. I write so that people can feel something for the small things. After a reading in Amman once, someone in the audience came up and asked me: 'Why are your poems full of animals?' And I didn't know what to answer because I had never thought about it or noticed it myself. Without thinking about it, I was functioning as some kind of ancient shaman, playing with animal masks and ritual dances. I was following in the steps of people who danced across the world perhaps 20,000 years ago—incredible! We repeat these things because we are forced to repeat them. And that goes to show that poetry and art are important. The need to create is an incredibly deep urge in me and people as a whole. I believe that humanity produces art by force; art is not something that only comes from within individual artists. An Arab poet was once asked why he wrote poetry and he replied, 'When your lungs are sick, you have to cough.'"

Muhammad throws open his hands and gives a faint smile: "And that's what I do, I cough."

Fuck Arafat!

Muhammad tells me that he has, as he puts it, made himself a new dictionary. So what does this dictionary look like? Have individual words—words like sex, for instance—been censored? Does he feel free to express himself as a writer in Palestine?

"Not always, no. Particularly not with regards to journalism, which is a real balancing act here. But my own experience shows that the Palestinian authorities are not the ones I should be afraid of, it's the people that scare me, this conservative society. I haven't always been as careful in my writing, and that has gotten me into trouble on many occasions. The leaning toward conservatism has become stronger over the past 25 years, maybe because people feel threatened. That's when you look for things that are solid and indisputable, because you don't trust what is new."

"You mean, only God is stronger than the Israeli tanks?"

"No, not God, but history. It has always been the case that when people feel threatened, they look for reassurance in the past."

"The literary critic Hassan Khader told me that there are three general taboos in Palestinian and Arabic literature, and they are sex, religion, and politics. Do you agree?"

"Not with the last one. You can write what you like about politics because there is no real authority here. You could shout

'Fuck Arafat!' in all the cafés, if you wanted. It's not the same here as is in Jordan, Egypt, or Syria. So when it comes to politics, we're free, with the exception of a handful of particular issues. Sex, that's one of them. But religion is the single most important topic that you have to avoid. I firmly believe that this insane version of Islam that we're experiencing now is a product of the US and its allies. The US supported the religious rebellion in Egypt in the early 1970s in order to crush Nasser and his Arab nationalism, and they supported similar movements in many other Arab countries, not least Afghanistan. And that's something that we—and you—are being punished for now. When I was young, we had one fundamentalist in our village, and he was totally isolated. Everyone ridiculed him."

"And now there are fundamentalists in every village."

"Yes. Hamas is thriving. Sometimes I feel that Israel actually welcomes it, because they couldn't repress us in the way they do if it weren't for the suicide bombers."

Muhammad points out that the majority of Palestinian writers are secular. He doesn't believe that a fundamentalist could be a good writer. He could perhaps write about religious or historical topics, but not about modern society. A writer, for Muhammad, is someone who observes society and himself from the outside. Religious fundamentalists, on the contrary, always have to be on the inside.

I ask him how this tallies with the fact that so many Palestinian authors are—or have been—involved in the Palestinian Authority and that so many of them work for the Ministry of Culture, in particular.

Muhammad has also worked in the Ministry of Culture. When he returned from exile in 1994, no one in Palestine knew him; no one knew that he was a writer and what he could do.

"I used my first three years back here to re-establish myself in society. I had to work for the Ministry of Culture, otherwise I wouldn't have been able to feed my children. Later, when I could perhaps have found another job, the second intifada erupted, and then there were no jobs to be had. Over the past three years, my salary has been halved. I now live on 850 US dollars a month, and of that, 500 goes to rent and 200 to regular expenses like water and gas. So all in all, my family survives on my wife's wages, which are 700 dollars a month."

"But you don't find there's a conflict of interest working with the authorities? What about your integrity?"

"There are no real, established authorities here, or at least, no authorities that can actually do anything. It's more like a kind of anarchy. But maybe you're right, maybe it does have an effect, I've never really given it much thought before. The point is that as an intellectual and writer, the choice is between working for the authorities or for a non-governmental organization [NGO]. There are no other alternatives. No proper publishing houses, research centers, newspapers, or magazines—certainly not where I could have a regular column and actually make a living from it. NGOs are also financially dependent on Western governments, so that would involve other ideological tripwires. Working with them might also have influenced my integrity. The question is, who needs writers? It is impossible to survive as a writer here, only Darwish can do that."

Indestructible Core

Two young women sitting at the table next to us suddenly burst into free and delightful laughter. Their two male companions laugh too. Melodic Arabic pop sings out over the tables from invisible speakers. Cars stream through the evening on the main road outside. It is dark now and I start to think about getting back to Jerusalem. No one wants to go through the Kalandia checkpoint after dark, if they can avoid it. No one knows when the checkpoint actually closes because it varies from night to night. I take another sip of juice.

Muhammad smiles and asks me what I think of Ramallah. And what about Israel? What had happened at the airport? He then asks me about my work, about what sort of things I write and what I am trying to achieve with my novels.

Muhammad is a man who prefers to listen, rather than talk. To ask questions, rather than answer them. Evening deepens outside the window. I work my way through his questions and then turn the discussion back to him: "You mentioned history earlier, and the fact that people look to history. Is the Arab heritage important to you?"

"Yes, absolutely. I am a product of that heritage, and classical Arabic poetry is of particular importance to me, as a poet. Although poetry has changed radically over the years, I'm still very closely attached to it; there is a continuity there, despite the fact that there has been a revolution."

"What about the Qur'an, is that also important to you?"

"As a piece of literature, yes. It is an incredibly beautiful book. And mythology and linguistics are important to me. I see myself as being half Palestinian, with an Arab cultural heritage, and half European intellectual. It can be a very fertile mix, but also rather complex."

"You mean that Palestine is linked to both Europe and the Arab world?"

"Yes, I think it is. Historically, the Arab world has always been very closely linked to Europe. And still is today. I don't think that there are any real barriers, I don't think there is an east and a west in the Mediterranean. But the prolific growth in fundamentalism over the past 25 years has caused some major changes."

"So, what constitutes a Palestinian? Is it at all possible to talk about a specific Palestinian identity?"

"Yes, I think it is. It is a voluntary identity, one that comes from the people, and not from above as in so many other Arab countries. Our literature has played an important role in forming this identity. Because Palestinian literature has been so successful in establishing a Palestinian identity, we are now free to leave politics behind. There is no danger if we eject politics from poetry. We are free to go other places, to talk about ants and stones or whatever we like. So as far as Palestinian identity is concerned, there is an inner core that is indestructible, by virtue of the fact that it is voluntary."

"So what is that core?"

"Well, it doesn't have a name. It's more a kind of feeling in people, and it always flourishes in difficult situations. You know, most people here don't like Arafat. They are sick and tired of him. But whenever they feel he is being threatened, they're the first to protect him. Because he symbolizes them, their feelings, identity, and rights."

"A feeling of having legitimate demands, that this place is theirs?"

"Yes. No Palestinian would ever question the fact that we are here. We haven't just arrived here, we've been here since ancient times. And perhaps that is why we're not quite as on our guard as the Israelis are. They feel they are the newcomers, so they have to be wary all the time. And that could be to their advantage. Maybe our sense of belonging makes us lazy."

A Shared Foundation

This feels like a natural point to raise our sights and look at the relationship between Israel and Palestine. And more specifically, at the potential role that literature could play in the conflict. I mention André Brink's experiences from South Africa, and ask Muhammad if he could imagine a similar development here.

"Yes, I really hope to see that happening here too. But the situation is different. In South Africa, the blacks and the whites wanted to build a country together."

"The intellectuals, that is."

"Yes. Personally, I would happily try to build a country together with David Grossman. I'm ready to meet Israeli writers any time. And I certainly read their work, even though we're not personal friends, but reading is my way of relating to the enemy. When it comes to translation, surely the whole point is to translate the best literature, as literature. I've read as much Israeli literature as I can, but as I said, we are denied access to things here, including Israeli literature, and it's not always easy to find English translations either."

In addition to translation, Muhammad talks passionately about teaching the other side's literature in schools. Does he believe that it's possible to learn something about the other side through their literature?

"Reading can give you a kind of understanding of the enemy, you recognize his motives and fears. I can sympathize with the Jews and their terrible experiences. We are all human beings. We can find common ground, like love, or life and death. And what's more, the Bible and the old Jewish teachings are also *my* heritage. Our ancestors all lived in this area, Jews included. I have more Jewish blood in my veins than Sharon."

"Really?"

"Yes, because our ancestors have lived here since pagan times. The Israelites converted to Judaism and then when Christianity was established, most of them converted to Christianity, and some even later to Islam. But basically it's the same people. When Jewish immigrants started coming here in the 1890s, they were truly astonished: 'Oh, these are the biblical people!' And it's true, we *are* the biblical people."

"Do you know any Israeli writers?"

"I don't have contact with many, on a personal level. I've only met two or three. And I wouldn't really say that we were friends. Perhaps because I'm quite isolated as a writer; I like to be on my own. But I do still think that we have to meet and to read each other's work. I don't think they know much about our culture. They think of our poetry in terms of the 1970s, as political junk food, and they have no idea about newer trends. So if the Israelis really believe that our common enemy is fanaticism, Hamas and Sharon, then we have to unite against it. Personally, I feel much closer to Grossman than I do to Sheikh Yassin, the spiritual leader of Hamas,[2] but the truth is that Israel oppresses me to the point where they almost force me to join Hamas. During the incursion last year, they stormed every single house in the town. They weren't after Hamas, they were after all of us, and the message I got was: you will get nothing more than I am willing to give you. And let me tell you something, I don't like living here. If the situation settles down and there's peace, I'm going to pack my bags and leave. But I won't leave now, because that would mean that I accept their victory over me and my people. It's a matter of principle. So, for the moment, I choose to stay here, even though I'm not happy."

The Jew as a Soldier

"I would be interested to hear about your image of the other side, how the Jew is portrayed in Palestinian literature?"

"Very badly. Or rather, nearly not at all. Because most people don't know Jews as anything other than soldiers. The people who really were in contact with the Israelis and who used to go there to work are not the people who write books."

"But you could perhaps talk to them, interview them?"

Muhammad thinks about it and then nods slowly.

"Yes, that's actually what we should do. The problem is that we have so many tasks ahead. I'm writing a historical book at the moment, even though I'm not a historian. It's a kind of duty, because no one else is writing about the old Philistines."

Muhammad nods thoughtfully when I mention Izzat Ghazzawi's lament about the lack of shared myths.

"Yes, you're right. We don't know very much about each other. No doubt their intelligence services know a lot about us, but not most ordinary people, not the intellectuals. There are lots of hurdles to get over, but there has to be a shared foundation. We have to agree to end this occupation, and either to have two states for two peoples, that is, an independent Palestinian state alongside Israel, or one state for two peoples. That has to be the basis on which we start talking to each other. There are so many things here that need to be discussed, not least the settlers. Most people in the West don't understand what the settler issue is all about. It means that anyone in the world can convert to Judaism one day and then come down here the next day and settle wherever they like, not only in Israel, but also here in the West Bank. They can buy some land in the vicinity of Ramallah and build themselves a house, which the Israelis will then immediately protect with checkpoints and soldiers. I have a friend who has always lived here in the West Bank, and he worked out how much time he has spent at checkpoints. Try to guess! Seven years! Seven wasted years!"

Not long after, I am standing at a checkpoint. No line, no one else is out this late at night. The Israeli soldiers let me pass without too many questions. There are no sherut taxis on the other side because it is late. I stand waiting for nearly half an hour. When a sherut taxi does finally appear and drive back, it's only half full. I sit in the front with the driver, who tells me with great passion why Kanafani[3] is so important to him and his life. A while later, he suddenly puts on his seatbelt and pulls over to the side of the road for some more Israeli soldiers. I decide to put on my seat belt as well. And that's what I'm fiddling with when the beam from the flashlight hits my face. I freeze, turn my head, and look straight into the muzzle of an Israeli rifle.

He could pull the trigger, but he doesn't. Instead he asks to see my passport, asks me where I'm staying, where I'm from and where I'm going. Not long after, we drive off again. The driver laughs off the whole incident: "That certainly made you jump!"

NOTES

1 In Jayyusi, ed., *Anthology of Modern Palestinian Literature* (1992), translated by Lena Jayyusi and Jeremy Reed. When I interviewed Muhammad in Ramallah in October 2003, he told me that the poem "Apology" was written in 1978.

2 Yassin was killed (along with nine civilians) by the Israeli military in a "targeted assassination" in Gaza in March 2004.

3 Ghassan Kanafani (1936–1972) is regarded as one of the best, if not *the* best, Palestinian prose writer. His work includes five novels, five collections of short stories, and two plays. Kanafani was born in Acre (today in Israel) in 1936 and lived in exile after 1948. He was a political activist and was killed by a car bomb in Beirut in 1972.

12

We have to be humane in our fight

Yahya Yakhlif

Yahya Yakhlif is an old hand in terms of Palestinian cultural life. He has written novels and has worked with culture and cultural policy both in exile and since his return to Ramallah in 1994.

At the time of writing, Yahklif was the Palestinian minister of culture. Before this, he was head of the Supreme Council of Education and Culture, a Fatah organization[1] that focuses on developing an effective cultural policy for the future. This was the position he had when I was in Israel in October 2003, though rumors were rife that he would be appointed as the new minister of culture.

With his cultural and political background, I thought that Yakhlif would be an excellent person with whom to discuss Palestinian literature and culture.

I dial his number from a shabby telephone kiosk in the center of Ramallah. When I called a week ago, he was in Paris attending various cultural meetings, but was due back around now, and according to his secretary, he would be more than happy to meet me. And sure enough, Yakhlif suggests in a resonant voice that we meet at the Grand Park Hotel, just outside the center of town. After asking for directions several times, the taxi driver manages to find this new hotel. A British TV crew is interviewing a besuited Palestinian man (a minister, perhaps) in the lobby. I don't have to wait long before two men come in through the door and approach me: "Are you here to meet Yahya Yakhlif?"

They have a car waiting outside, so I follow them out. Shortly after, we stop in front of a newly erected building and take the elevator up to a well-equipped office, where Yakhlif greets me, all smiles and impeccably dressed. The driver sits down too. He will apparently be staying with us for the interview, largely as an interpreter (Yakhlif does not speak fluent English), but also, as it turns out, as a commentator.

Taboo and censorship—I am interested to hear what shape these take for a man like Yakhlif, who has some real cultural clout and actually exercises it. Are there things that he cannot or does not want to write about?

To begin with, he doesn't understand my question. The driver asks me to repeat it, and then leans forward and explains to Yakhlif, who clears his throat and chuckles.

"Well, there are normally three taboos in the Arab world: politics, sex, and religion."

"And is it possible to create good literature with those kinds of restrictions?"

"You can still write the novel you want to write. You may not get it published everywhere, but you can always have it published in, say, Beirut, which is very liberal."

"But the Egyptian Nobel laureate Naguib Mahfouz published a novel in Beirut and was later almost assassinated in Cairo because some religious fundamentalists found something they didn't like. Could something similar happen here, even if the book was published in Beirut?"

"No, there are no problems like that here. People are usually sent to prison for political reasons, not because of a novel."

"Some Palestinian writers have told me that they don't write about religion at all because they're worried about the fundamentalists, who just keep gaining ground and power."

The words hang in the air for a moment before Yakhlif answers: "Only once since the Palestinian Authority was established in 1994 has a book been stopped. It was a book by Edward Said [see chapter 9, note 4] and it was stopped by the intelligence services. But we resolved the problem straight away. In fact, I went to Abu Ammar [Arafat] myself and asked him what the fuss was all about. He had no idea about what had happened and said to me: 'You can allow any book to come into Palestine and be published. No problem.' Because these days, you can read any book you like on the internet, so you can't prevent the publication of books anymore."

Not the Right Climate

A woman comes in with a platter of freshly cut fruit and puts it down on the table between us. The telephone rings on Yakhlif's desk and he gets up. The driver smiles and asks me to help myself to fruit. While I enjoy a piece of refreshing melon, I try to follow through a line of thought: the Oslo Accords facilitated a political situation whereby the PLO can now have discussions with Israel. And Fatah is a part of the PLO. And Yakhlif is a member of Fatah. Does that then mean that he, as a writer or a politician, is in some way engaged in a dialogue with any Israeli writers or with Israeli literature?

Yakhlif puts down the receiver and comes back to the sofa. He shakes his head. "It is very difficult to talk about peace with the people who are occupying your country. If you're going to have an equal relationship, then you have to have two independent parties. OK, so some left-wing Israelis declare from time to time that they're opposed to the occupation, but then later say that the Jewish settlements should remain on Palestinian land, or they ask Palestinian writers to stop campaigning for the rights of the 1948 refugees. Israeli writers are as slippery as oil, you can't get hold of them from any angle. We will talk to the Israeli intellectuals when our country is free, but it is not possible to have a true dialogue between victim and oppressor."

I argue that the situation in South Africa also involved victims and an oppressor, but André Brink still believes that literature, and the fact that black and white authors started to read each other's work, was a powerful force in the work to dismantle the apartheid regime.

"In South Africa there were many whites who fought alongside the blacks for freedom and humanity, but in Israel there are only a handful of exceptions, the odd journalist or peace activist."

"What about well-known authors like Amos Oz and David Grossman?"

"Amos Oz stands somewhere between the left and right. Grossman is the only important writer I can think of, off the top of my head, who genuinely acknowledges the rights of the Palestinians. He also writes very well about Palestinians in his novels."

I ask how it works the other way around. How does Yakhlif see the Jew/Israeli being portrayed in Palestinian literature?

"The Israelis are our enemy! But on the whole, Palestinian literature is very human. I have met many writers from abroad who have told me that they only really started to understand the Palestinian question when they read work by Palestinian writers such as Kanafani. He writes about Palestinian suffering, and there is something deeply human about his books. In general, you could say that the Israeli is a soldier in Palestinian literature. But we don't write about the Israelis as animals, in the way that the Israelis write about others."

"I get the impression that one of the major problems here, for many people, is that it is very difficult to see the other side. If you were to read Israeli literature, would it then be possible to see that they too have feelings, problems, doubts, etc.?"

"That is a very big problem, my friend. The Jewish people came to our country. They came and established Israel and behaved as if we were slaves and they were the rulers. Their democracy applies to the Jewish people, not to the Palestinians—nor to the Arabs who live in Israel. Israel is an apartheid state, and we sincerely hope that one day Israeli society will change."

"What you're saying is that there has to be a political solution first, and then literature may be able to play a role?"

"A political solution first, yes. Then culture can be used as a catalyst to bring people together, so they can work together and be good neighbors. Let us hope! Because the truth is that we, both Jews and Palestinians, will carry on living here in this area until the end of time. But they *have to* respect our rights: an independent and recognized state with the 1967 borders. A lot of things will change in the future, when there is peace."

"But something *is* happening on the literary front, isn't it? One of your own short stories has been translated into Hebrew and published in an anthology in Israel."

"Yes, but that's more of an exception than the rule. Israel translates very little Arabic literature into Hebrew. A few novels by the Egyptian Naguib Mahfouz, that's it. They're not interested in Arabic literature."

"Two of Darwish's collections have been translated into Hebrew."

"Yes, that is true, but it's still not normal. We translate a lot more from Hebrew than they do from Arabic."

"What about Palestinian school books, do they include Israeli writers?"

"No, but that will change as soon as we've established an independent Palestinian state. Then we'll find the courage to shout, 'We have to learn to understand these people! Let's talk to them!' But no one can talk now, when all we see is tanks and bombs and people getting killed all the time. This is not the right climate for talking."

Myths of Harmony

The telephone rings and Yakhlif excuses himself once more. The driver smiles and offers me some more fruit. Yakhlif puts the phone down, finds a remote control and switches on the Arabic TV station al-Jazeera. He and the driver exchange a few words. On the TV screen, I see ambulances with flashing blue lights and confused people. A burnt-out car. I carefully ask what has happened. The driver calmly confirms that there has been another bomb attack, in Gaza this time. They don't know all the details yet, but it appears that some Americans have died. He turns to look at the screen. "Four Americans killed," he says, a moment later. "It seems that the bombs were buried under the road and detonated by remote control."

American lives. What will happen now? Elementary math and the logic of war would say a swift and brutal retaliation by Israel. The first step is usually to close the borders. Will this be a repeat of what happened in spring 2002, when everything exploded on the very night that I touched down in the so-called Holy Land? But back then, I was a free man in Israel. Now I could be caught on the Palestinian side, surrounded by Israeli tanks that crush anything in their way. I have to get to the Kalandia checkpoint and cross over to Israel as quickly as possible.

"Do you think they will close Kalandia?" I ask, hesitantly.

Yakhlif lights another cigarette and shrugs, indicating that it is one possibility of many. The driver reckons that nothing will happen for the next hour or two. Both of them are completely calm. They have seen all this before. Heard it all before. This is reality—for them. Not for me. A few minutes later Yakhlif turns the television off. It's time to get on with the interview.

I have a little list of questions with me and plump for the first one my eyes fall on: "Has Palestinian literature changed since 1994 when the PLO and a host of Palestinian authors came back after years in exile?"

"After the Oslo Accords many writers and intellectuals came back, and they really invigorated the cultural life here. So before September 2000, when the second intifada started, we actually had a very active cultural life, with theater, music, and art. An infrastructure was built up, with museums and art centers. And now there has been a real backlash. We're not allowed to import books anymore, neither Arabic nor English. They have demolished the museums and parts of the old towns, as in Nablus. Several cultural events have had to be cancelled because of this aggression. But, in spite of the terrible situation, Palestinian intellectuals are still trying to create room for hope; they try to carry on painting, making music and theater—and writing. Many Palestinian authors are now writing about their new life in Palestine, as well as striving to highlight universal values and what it means to be part of the human race. But if you want to know about trends in recent literature, it may be a bit early to say. You may have to wait five or ten years to discover what this new literature looks like."

"And how have you developed as a writer, yourself, since 1994?"

"I've written lots of books about life in Palestine and life in exile. After I came back in 1994, I wrote a novel about an experience I had here.[2] It's about a journey from Gaza to the village of Samakh by Lake Tiberias (now in Israel), where I was born in 1944. The village was destroyed in 1948 when the Israelis occupied the whole area. I was four years old, and we fled to Jordan, where I grew up in a refugee camp. I was trying to imagine what actually happened back then. So I traveled back to Samakh 46 years later and then wrote a novel about it. There aren't even any ruins there because the Israelis built their houses on top of our old ones. All that's left are a few bits of the old railway station. I wanted to see the place where I grew up, but I was also looking for an old Jewish lady. Before 1948, she worked in a nightclub and fell in love with a Palestinian called Khatura. In 1948, Khatura was forced to flee and ended up in a refugee camp in Damascus. This Jewish woman followed him and lived with him in the refugee camp. When the Syrian authorities discovered that she was a Jew, she was put in prison. And then when they realized it was a love story, she was sent back to Israel."

"Was the Palestinian man allowed to return as well?"

Yakhlif gives a wide, almost patronizing grin.

"No. Israel did not let him back in, so he stayed in Damascus. But they wrote to each other. He died about ten years later. And she kept the memory of him in her heart. When I went to Lake Tiberias about eight years ago, I had a friend with me who was related to Khatura. We looked for the woman, and after two days we found her. She was very old, deaf and dumb with a wrinkled face. I wrote a novel about the experience."

So, am I to understand that it is a novel about a Jewish–Palestinian friendship, even a love affair? I mention Ghazzawi's thoughts about the lack of stories of understanding between Jews and Palestinians. Yakhlif nods. "Of course there are no such stories, because of the situation."

"But your latest novel, about the relationship between Khatura and the Jewish woman, is precisely that."

"It's a true story. Before 1948, the Palestinians had good

relations with the Jews. In our village, we all went to a Jewish doctor when we were ill. Some of the Jews came to celebrate our Muslim festivals with us, as a mark of respect. But after 1948 and all the aggression, there was a deep divide between the two people."

"Would it be correct to say that many of you, both Jews and Palestinians, have good memories of the times before 1948, but that it's difficult to write about these now, because of the occupation?"

"No, you *can* write about them. Why not? Lots of Palestinians have written about things like that."

Prior to 1948, Samakh was part of the British Mandate of Palestine, and after 1948, it became part of Israel. The village is also central to some of Yakhlif's earlier novels. In *A Lake Beyond the Wind* (1991), Samakh is described as a sleepy, charming village that is gradually overtaken by reality in 1947–1948. Several of the men from the village volunteer as soldiers, but it all ends in defeat, and ultimately, in exile. The last paragraph of the book says: "I realized then that everything had been lost, that all paths led to exile and dispersion. Such a melancholy prospect. Such a lonely road."

"Is the story very close to the truth of what happened?"

"Yes. It is the story of my family. I researched it for two years, and interviewed a lot of old people about what they remembered, because what happened in Samakh isn't recorded in any history books. I also studied the geography, found out about the fish in Lake Tiberias, and about the plants, birds, traditions, everything. But as a writer, I have of course changed a number of things."

"Your novel is far from heroic. These are just ordinary people, aren't they?"

"Yes. I wrote about people, about their strengths, but also their weaknesses. It's about how the whole drama began, how we lost our country and became refugees. It is a human drama."

If we look at the portrayal of Jews in the novel, what do we see? We see soldiers, which is of course not surprising. The novel is about *al-Nakba* (the catastrophe), as the Palestinians call it—or the war of liberation, as the Israelis call it. A number of the characters in the novel express their opinion of Jews, for example:

"The Jews are moving forward like locusts [...] eating everything, green or dry" or "If we don't stop them, they'll kill us and rip open our women's bellies."

The story recounts the fear and despair, the discussions and uncoordinated attempts to establish an effective Arab army. There is no heroism here. It is a novel about people and their preconceptions and fear of the enemy.

I recall a short scene from the town of Tiberias, which is teeming with life: "... there were all kinds of faces, Arab and Jew, and British police cars." No more than that. Just a brief aside that illustrates something that is so seldom mentioned in literature but comes to the fore again and again in my interviews: that in the past, Palestine was a place where all kinds of people lived together, Arabs and Jews and many others.

Identity and Loss

The novel ends with loss and exile, and that is still the reality for many, many Palestinians today. Exile and the memory of what has been lost. Given this, I ask Yakhlif about Palestinian identity. Is it now inextricably linked to a sense of loss?

"Of course. The novel is about the start of Palestinian suffering. Many people lost their land and home and became refugees. I remember only too well how much we suffered in those camps when I was a child. The winters were cold in those days, and many children died of hunger or hypothermia. I went to a UNRWA school, where they gave us a cup of milk every day and a fish-oil capsule, to help us. And they gave us blankets. I remember lots of details like that. It was 1948, just after the Second World War. Europe was trying to export the problem of the Jews here to the Middle East. So the Palestinians were also victims of the Second World War. We had to pay for the Jewish problem—even though we were not part of it. It was Germany—not the German people as such, but the Nazi government—who killed the Jews. Why should the Palestinians have to pay such a high price for that? The truth is that we lost our identity at that time. We had no government, no state, and were strangers in foreign countries. So it was culture that held the Palestinians together and it became one of the cornerstones of our identity. Palestinian literature united Palestinians both here in Palestine and elsewhere. Yes, culture played a very important role."

"Would you say that today's literature still plays a role in the national struggle and that it is therefore political?"

"No, not exactly political, though resistance is a driving force in the greater part of Palestinian literature. But standards are still high, in purely literary terms. Many Palestinian authors have won important prizes for their work."

The telephone rings again. Yakhlif excuses himself again, goes over to the desk and picks up the receiver. Not long after, he switches on the television again, al-Jazeera with the latest news about the bombs in Gaza. Yakhlif and the driver talk quietly to each other. More pictures of ambulances and screaming people fill the screen. The driver nods and smiles at me. "I think there might be a line at the Kalandia checkpoint today," he says. "Lots of people will want to get out while they can."

Terrorism. In one of Yakhlif's short stories, the characters discuss hijacking, among other things. I mention the short story. Yakhlif turns the television off.

"Of course I am opposed to terrorism, just like the characters in that short story. I do not condone the attacks that Hamas and [Islamic] Jihad carry out in Tel Aviv or wherever it may be, which affect civilians and innocent people. We have the right to fight against the occupation, but we do not have the right to kill civilians—that has absolutely nothing to do with our values as Palestinians, nor the values of Islam. The Prophet himself advised his military leaders: 'Do not kill old women. Do not kill children. Do not cut down trees.' There are values that we have to protect. And we have to be humane in our fight. The groups behind all these attacks are not a part of the true Islam. I am a Muslim, but I am not a member of Hamas. Arafat is a Muslim, he prays five times a day, but he is not a member of Hamas. When you start to mix religion and politics, you are headed down the wrong road."

Yakhlif leans forward and takes a piece of melon. "Religion is between you and God."

The interview is drawing to a close, and I am impatient to be on my way, to get through Kalandia and back to Jerusalem.

"Just one final question. Who will be the next Palestinian minister of culture?"

Yakhlif chuckles, gets up, and walks around the room. "My name has come up and I can only hope. But to be honest, I don't really want to be a minister. I am happy to be a writer, to pursue the cultural goals I have in mind. I have lots of projects and I believe that cultural projects are an essential part of the national project as a whole."

"What do you see as being the principle problem for Palestinian culture? Is it money?"

"There are lots of problems. Finance is one of them, but not the greatest. The main problem is the occupation. How can you initiate and work on projects in these difficult circumstances? How can you establish connections between Palestinian and Arab culture, between Palestinian culture and world culture? How can culture play an active role in supporting the Palestinian people? How can culture help open the door for the Palestinian people, the door to the world? Culture is an excellent ambassador for the Palestinians. You can't touch people's hearts with politics, but culture allows you to touch their hearts, minds, and souls."

"And what about Yakhlif the writer, do you find time to write at all, when you're so involved with cultural policy?"

"I see myself as an intellectual, not as an employee or a minister. I am proud of my identity as a writer. Time to write? *Ya'ani,* I don't have *enough* time, but I survive."

He sits down on the leather sofa, slaps his thigh and gives a hearty laugh: "I survive."

The driver takes me back to the center, and from there I immediately take a sherut taxi to Kalandia. The line is very long, very long. Many people want to get out. Israeli retribution is imminent. Of course, most people *cannot* get out, because their Palestinian ID cards imprison them in the West Bank and Gaza.

Within an hour I am through, and with every fiber in my body I appreciate how fortunate I am to be Norwegian.

NOTES

1 The Palestinian resistance organization al-Fatah was established in 1956 and was led by Arafat from 1964 until his death, when he was succeeded by leading Fatah member Mahmoud Abbas as Palestinian National Authority president. Fatah has been the dominant party under the umbrella organization PLO since 1969, the year when Arafat also became leader of the PLO (see also chapter 10, note 2), but suffered a major upset in January 2006 when it lost its parliamentary majority to Hamas. Conflict between Fatah and Hamas has dominated Palestinian politics since.

2 This novel, *Nahr yastahimmu fi al-buhayrah* (1997), has not been translated into any Western language. It is one of the very first novels to deal with the return to Palestine after years in exile.

13

Men dominate society

Sahar Khalifeh

Sahar Khalifeh is recognized as one of Palestine's leading writers today. Her breakthrough novel, in Palestine and internationally, was *Wild Thorns* (1976), which has been translated into a number of languages, including Hebrew. She is an outspoken feminist and an important figure in the fight for equality for Arab women. She is also the director of the Women's Affairs Center in Nablus, where she grew up. She now splits her time between her homes in Nablus in the West Bank and Amman, the capital of Jordan.

When I first went to the Middle East in spring 2002, my "fixer" Ghazzawi had not been able to get in touch with Khalifeh. The same thing happened in October 2003. Shuqair, who became my middleman in Palestine following the death of Ghazzawi, had not managed to track her down either. He gave me two telephone numbers, one in Nablus and the other in Amman. I rang them both, morning and evening, without luck. One morning when I was at Ogarit, the publishing house in Ramallah, the author and publisher Walid Abu Bakr smiled and told me that Khalifeh had just been there, in his office. But that she was probably on her way back to Amman now. So I dialed the number in Amman, again and again, and got nothing but the dial tone.

This chapter was only made possible by modern technology—email, that is. Back home again in Norway, the weeks ticked by; 2003 turned into 2004. I phoned Khalifeh again in Amman, and she answered the first time. She had had problems with her phone the previous autumn, but that was all sorted out now. She suggested that I send her my questions by email, and then she could answer them.

So that's what happened. I sent her my questions and she sent me her answers. I was particularly interested to see what she had to say about the status of Palestinian and Arab women today. What were she and other like-minded people fighting for? What was most needed? And were things moving in the right direction?

Her replies are short and concise, and in perfect English. She studied in the US and has a PhD both in women's studies and American literature from the University of Iowa.

"On the whole, the situation for Palestinian women today is just as it was. There have been no real changes, though there are of course more educated women, more female doctors, university lecturers, artists, and writers. But they come from the elite classes and live in a completely different world from the masses. The truth is that the Islamist movement has had a great influence on the masses over the past 30 years, and has robbed women of many of the few small victories that we had achieved. So what do we need? First and foremost, we need better political leadership, a leadership that takes women seriously and introduces laws that entail that women are treated as equals. Personally, I am working for liberation and human rights for all. Despite the many setbacks, I still believe that I have had a certain influence. I was the first feminist in the Arab world to write about women's issues in a literary form. I have had some influence on educated women, but I have not had much influence on men—and it is men who dominate society here, at all levels."

What are the greatest obstacles to equality for women?

"There are many, many obstacles in our way. The Israeli occupation, naturally. Our own traditional leadership. Poverty and illiteracy. There is also a dangerous lack of real communication and friendship with the Western world. The West views us with suspicion and we are suspicious of them. I think that communication between different cultures is essential to development. I myself have studied in the West, I have lived and worked there—and can, with my hand on my heart, say that I have no exaggerated dreams about Western culture. But I am absolutely convinced that the Western world has a lot to teach us. I only wish that you were not so biased, as then the world would be a better place. At least for us!"

As a feminist author, do you feel that you have a special responsibility?

"Well, the fact that I am a feminist author with a feminist vision of the world does of course make my literature very critical—and the criticism is targeted at both my own society and Israel. I can see that both societies are oppressive in different ways. The reality in which I find myself at any given time is extremely complex and that means that it is very difficult for me to write without watching every step I make. I cannot allow myself the luxury that other writers may have elsewhere; I cannot just rattle off something for no other reason than to satisfy my own feelings and dreams. I really feel that I represent my people, despite my critical views on our culture and many of its beliefs and values. So yes, I do feel a responsibility to change some of those beliefs and values. My position means that I am constantly in conflict with our traditional leaders, not just political, but also religious and social leaders."

Given that she is so critical of her own culture, does that mean that Arab cultural heritage means nothing to Khalifeh? And what about Islam? How does she define herself as a Palestinian?

Again, she replies in short, precise sentences, subdued and yet firm.

"I am a Palestinian writer who has suffered and is still suffering under this terrible Israeli occupation. I also feel frustrated by our own weakness, as Arabs in general and Palestinians in particular. Our culture does not mean that much to me. It is not sacred. I am very critical of it. It has to change. We cannot develop unless we are strong enough to face our own weakness, head on. And Islam, well, Islam is a part of our culture."

Literature and Conflict

I discern a very clear willingness to see the other side in Khalifeh's novels. *Wild Thorns* is about different ways of dealing with reality when you live under an occupation. The action takes place in Nablus in the 1970s, with two cousins at the center of a varied and polyphonic gallery of characters. One of them travels into Israel every day to work for a pittance, and the other becomes a dedicated freedom fighter. "His destiny was no longer a matter of personal choice or whim... he'd become a link in the chain of the cause."

I must just point out that the freedom fighter is called Usama—a strange precursor of the US war on global terrorism in general and Osama bin Laden in particular. Early on in the book, Usama stabs an Israeli officer, in front of the officer's wife and young daughter.

The reason that the novel was such an experience for me to read is that, time and again, it comes into conflict with itself, yet never once opts for black or white, but plays on a whole range of colors. One possible interpretation is that it is circumstances that decide whether a person becomes a murderer. But the book also says that people must fight for their humanity, despite their circumstances.

With hindsight—and in reality—we of course know that the first intifada broke out eleven years after the book was first published in 1976. You could read the book and say: hate doesn't grow out of nothing. If you look at what the occupation and Israeli oppression have done to the individual Palestinian, then the novel has probably the same message as *The Yellow Wind*, David Grossman's report from 1986: that the whole thing is about to explode.

However, Khalifeh does not agree that she portrays the Jew as a whole person.

"Israelis are always minor characters in my books. Why? Because in reality we only come into contact with soldiers and other representatives of the occupation. We have minimal contact with Israeli civilians. How can I write about somebody or something I don't really know? Despite my best intentions and feelings for them as fellow human beings, I can't capture them as full-rounded figures. After all, what is literature? It reflects life, society, and the people who live there. Not in the same way that a photograph does, of course, since the author's personal feelings and opinions will be blended in. An author also strives to transcend reality and make it more beautiful and valuable. You could say that I have one obligation in my writing and that is to reflect the lives of people living under the occupation. My literature is highly political, as our lives are dominated by politics. But it is not dry or rigid, as you might easily imagine. My characters are full of life. They are flesh and blood. You can feel them, smell them, and touch them."

No Common Ground

Khalifeh does not read much Hebrew literature because she has no access to it. And she is not sure what has happened to two of her novels that were translated into Hebrew and published in Israel. She writes to me that some left-wing Israelis had worked hard for her work to be translated, but she is not convinced that people on the streets of Tel Aviv would actually read them.

I wonder if she sees literature as a potential conciliator, along the lines of what happened in South Africa. Could Khalifeh imagine a similar process in the Middle East?

"I don't think so. All attempts to bring writers and artists, even feminists, from both sides together have failed. And why? Because the Israelis feel superior, rather than equal to us. That is one reason. The other is that they don't feel connected to the Third World in any way. They are connected with the first or the Western world. And third, they are deeply racist. So I ask myself, how can a person grow up in such an atmosphere without being infected? It isn't easy to deal with them. All previous attempts have failed."

What about literature, then—what about translating and reading their literature? Could that be a way?

As I read her final words, I can almost feel her hand shaking as she writes.

"Without any real solution at a political level, all this talk of translation and conferences and meetings with the other side will come to nothing. Many attempts have been made over the years, but nothing has helped. So what is the best thing to do now? Well, the best thing would be to concentrate our energy on finding a tenable solution that could bring peace to the region, instead of wasting time on wishful thinking and all sorts of experiments. The truth is that there is a complete divide between us and them, geographically, politically, and culturally. The only Israelis we Palestinians have any contact with are the soldiers. That is the reality. We have no common ground."

14

It is our duty to know about the other side

Mahmoud Darwish and Izzat Ghazzawi

M ahmoud Darwish is without a doubt the most well-
known and acclaimed of all contemporary Palestinian
writers. He was primarily a poet, but also wrote
memoirs and a number of essays and articles. It would be no
exaggeration to say that he was regarded as a hero and was elevated
to the status of living legend. He was also Palestine's national poet.[1]

From the start of this project, I knew that it was essential for
me to meet certain authors: David Grossman and Amos Oz on the
Israeli side, and Izzat Ghazzawi and Mahmoud Darwish on the
Palestinian side.

When I arrived in Israel in spring 2002, I had arranged a
meeting with Darwish. Then all hell broke loose. No one, except
Israeli soldiers and tanks, could get into the West Bank, and the
people who were already there were kept under house arrest.

My original plan was to do all the interviews with both Israeli
and Palestinian writers in one go in spring 2002. This was of course
not possible. So I had to plan another trip. This time I wanted to
have all the meetings arranged before I booked my ticket—which
I managed to do. Early October looked good for everyone. I was
assured that even Darwish would be Ramallah.

I arrived in Jerusalem full of renewed enthusiasm on the last
day of September 2003. I checked in to the same hotel where I
had stayed on my previous visit, a converted monastery in the old
Christian quarters. When I spoke to Shuqair on the phone, he
thought that maybe Darwish had gone to Amman, and suggested
that I call his secretary. When I called the next morning, his

secretary informed me: "Darwish is abroad and will not be back until next year." I said that I would happily go to Amman to meet him there, if that was at all possible. The secretary coughed and said that she in fact didn't know where he was. A few days later I was in Ramallah to meet Hassan Khader, who runs the periodical *Al-Karmel* together with Darwish. And he told me that Darwish was in Germany, on his way to Istanbul to receive a literary prize, and that he would fly directly from there to Paris. "He'll stay in Paris over the autumn. He lived in Paris for many years, you know, and likes to spend some time there every year when he's writing."

Back home in Norway, I tried again and again, through both Khader and Shuqair, to arrange a meeting with Darwish in Paris sometime before Christmas. To this day, I am still not sure what happened, or more to the point, why nothing happened. I was told that Darwish was constantly hounded by journalists wherever he went and that every now and then, especially when he was writing, he needed to isolate himself for periods, to protect himself.

I was forced to give up. However, Darwish has written so much about his own work and on a number of the topics that I wanted to raise with him that I can, with a somewhat heavy heart, refer those who are interested to the bibliography. In his essay "Palestine: the Imaginary and the Real," which he wrote in 2000, he raises a number of questions about the role of the writer and literature, and his own role as a poet.

Darwish has for many years highlighted the necessity of cultural dialogue between the Israelis and the Palestinians. In this essay, he makes an interesting distinction between the concepts knowledge, dialogue, and normalization. "Knowledge of the other (i.e. the Israeli) is an indisputable cultural obligation. We have to know the Israeli in order to know how to compromise with him or how to fight against him. The image of the Israeli in the Arab consciousness is an abstract and prototypical one that is at odds with the requirements of cultural knowledge," he writes.

Israelis and Palestinians share a common future, and therefore dialogue between the two parties is imperative. Darwish emphasizes that dialogue with the Israelis is nothing to be ashamed of. "On the contrary, such a dialogue enriches me, for it enhances my knowledge of myself when my destiny and that of the other converge."

Darwish also considers the meaning of cultural normalization. A culture cannot be forced into a relationship with another culture; it has to happen as and when the need arises. "On the one hand, the Arab culture does not need to learn from Hebrew culture; nor does it have to fear it, on the other. Dialogue among cultures is a much greater topic than the political issue."

The fact is that, according to Darwish, the Israelis have not shown any interest in cultural dialogue. "Normalization, for them, lies outside culture. It lies at the security, political, and economic levels."

The essay therefore ends with the following (political) conclusion by Darwish: "In this context, I do not hesitate to declare my rejection of the issue of normalization as long as the causes for boycott still exist. And as long as the Palestinian land and some Arab lands are still occupied, relations between the Arabs and the Israelis will not be normal. The Arab boycott against Israel has to continue so as to let the Israelis realize that peace is, at least, in their own interest."

This three-way strategy of knowledge, dialogue, and normalization is worth noting. It could possibly help to resolve the eternal chicken-and-egg problem that runs throughout this book, i.e., the relationship between literature on the one hand and the conflict on the other. What should come first? Is a political solution needed first, before literature can play a role? Or should literature come first—as a force that can help guide policy or lay the foundations for political solutions?

Knowledge and dialogue are imperative, according to Darwish. But normalization is a completely different issue that can only happen when the political issue—the Israeli occupation of Arab land—is resolved.

I had also prepared myself to quiz Darwish about the portrayal of the other side in his own literature. I particularly wanted to ask him about Rita, a Jewish woman who is the subject of several of his poems and whom he wrote about with fascination, delight, and desire. A Palestinian man and an Israeli woman, together, even sexually. An incredible scenario indeed.

"Rita and the Rifle" is a retrospective, looking back at a relationship with Rita: "And I kissed Rita / When she was young / And I remember how she hung on / To me and covered my arm with the loveliest braid [...] Rita's name was a feast in my mouth / Rita's body was a wedding in my blood / And for two years I was lost in Rita / And for two years she slept on my arms."

This is about a Palestinian man's passion for an Israeli woman. A relationship that did not last, however.

Even though I didn't meet Darwish and so couldn't ask him in person about the Rita poems, I did talk about them on several occasions with other people, such as when I met Mahmoud Shuqair in East Jerusalem in October 2003. I asked him why Darwish keeps returning to a Jewish Israeli woman in his poems. Is there some kind of fascination here vis-à-vis the other side?

Shuqair explained: "Darwish was born in Israel and grew up there. He knows Israeli society inside out. Rita was a real woman who he fell in love with, but as he writes in one of the Rita poems: 'Between Rita and my eyes... a rifle,' in other words, the conflict, the current situation. But he pours all his human emotions and passions into this woman, that is true."

The literary critic Hassan Khader believes that a form of ambiguous fascination with the other side does exist between the Israelis and the Palestinians. "Even though we are enemies and kill each other, you constantly discover that there are things that we have in common. In any international gathering of people, we recognize each other instantly. Sexual fantasies in relation to the other side are not unusual in Israeli literature. It is unusual in our literature, but only because sex in general is not talked about openly. Darwish is in a category of his own. He constantly expresses his fascination with the other side. And not only in his earlier poems, he still does it today. Rita, or the image of the other, is always there."

In my dialogue with the Israeli author Dorit Rabinyan, I mentioned Darwish and Rita. She beamed at me: "Is that true? Has he really written poems like that? Could you send me copies of some of them? Please. It's very important to me."

Izzat Ghazzawi had a very special relationship with Norway. Unfortunately, he died in spring 2003, when he was only 52. He died of a heart attack in his home in Ramallah. I and several other Norwegian authors had met him many times, and we were in regular contact via email in the last years of his life. Even though we discussed a great many issues during our brief meetings, or by mail or on the phone, I never actually interviewed him. When I first visited the region in April 2002, I talked to him on the phone now and then. Like the rest of Ramallah, he was subject to a strict curfew, but was as optimistic as ever and believed that the situation would be resolved soon. During that period, he submitted a series of articles to the Norwegian newspaper *Dagbladet* under the heading "Diary from Ramallah," giving Norwegian readers a unique insight into the Palestinian reality.

The next time that I was in the region in autumn 2003, Ghazzawi was no longer with us.

In addition to being an author, he was a professor at Birzeit University, a director of Ogarit Publishers, and the chairman of the Palestinian Writers' Union. He was also writing a doctoral dissertation on modern Israeli and Palestinian literature.

Ghazzawi was a man of peace and reconciliation, in both word and deed. He first came to Norway in 1993, when the Norwegian Authors' Union initiated a meeting between Israeli and Palestinian writers. He later said that the meeting between the Israeli and Palestinian writers in June was in many ways a manifestation of the fact that peace could only be created through understanding and by people meeting each other and talking.[2]

But in order to be able to understand each other through literature, the other side's literature has to be available. As a director of Ogarit, Ghazzawi was involved in the translation and publication of Hebrew literature in Palestine. He met Etgar Keret at the Kapittel Festival of Literature and Freedom of Speech in Stavanger in 2002, and as a result of this meeting, Keret was translated into Arabic and published in Ramallah.

Ghazzawi was also in close contact with Israeli authors such as David Grossman and Amos Oz, and constantly emphasized the need for dialogue with Israeli writers and intellectuals. "We write letters to each other where we discuss what we as artists can and should do in the dangerous situation in which we live," he said in an interview in 1997.[3]

When David Grossman visited Norway in 1995, he attended a meeting in the Mosiac Religious Community in Oslo. Here he was challenged by a Norwegian Jew who claimed that his peace work was in fact giving stones to the enemy, and that there was not a single Arab author who writes books about peace with Israel in the way that Grossman writes about peace with the Arabs. Grossman replied: "I can give you several names. One of them, Izzat al-Ghazzawi, recently received a prize in this country [The Norwegian Authors' Union's Freedom of Expression Prize in 1994]. He was originally a member of the PLO, but he decided to invest his energy in peace instead. Around this time, his son was killed by our soldiers, close to their home. In spite of this, he made it clear at the funeral that he would continue to fight for peace. Last summer he was elected as the chairman of the Palestinian Writers' Union. Which goes to show that his vision is legitimate."[4]

Three of Ghazzawi's works were translated into Norwegian while he was still alive. *Letters Underway* was the first. It is not a novel as such, but rather a kind of diary, written by the author when he was in prison in Israel from 1988 to 1990. In it, Ghazzawi says: "We also have to write to our own people, our wives and children, our friends and to the other people who live around us. Our song must be sung in two languages simultaneously, or we will lose our home forever. You know, we share our house with the Jewish people, and we must ensure that no one demands the whole house, and throws the others out into the cold."

These words are unambiguous. The Palestinians and the Jews share the same house.

Ghazzawi's novel *The Truth is Sleeping* was his fourth work to be translated into Norwegian, posthumously. It is in many ways a daring novel. The greater part of the novel comprises a manuscript found by a son after his father has died, a manuscript about the Sufi Husayn Ibn Mansour al-Hallaj (857–922), a well-known figure in Arabic and Islamic history.

I interpret Husayn to be a kind of religious model. He talks of moderation, respect for the individual, and equality. God lives in us all, whether we acknowledge this or not. This respect and equality is in no way linked to race (e.g., Arabs) or religion (e.g., Islam), but is universal. All religions spring from the same source, Husayn preached, and are basically different representations of one and the same God. And the essence of this God is love, not punishment. Tolerance is a key concept in his teachings.

I read this as a message. I think that Ghazzawi must have written this novel with the hope of highlighting another side of Islam—not another Islam—and showing that Islam already contains what is needed to enter a new era.

Notes

1 Darwish passed away as the English edition of this book was being prepared, on August 9, 2008, at the age of 67.

2 Steien (1994).

3 Gustavsen (1997).

4 Morken (1995).

15

Or should we do something about it?
An Israeli–Palestinian Contribution

Salman Natour

As I mentioned in the introduction to this book, I was forced early on to set limits—quite simply, to make exclusions. The book was to include only *living* writers who reside and work in Israel or Palestine. I wanted them to have this proximity to and experience of the conflict. At the same time, this meant excluding interesting Palestinian writers who live abroad, such as Anton Shammas (see chapter 1, note 10), who lives in the US, and Mourid Barghouti,[1] who lives in Egypt. In addition, I chose not to include a number of Palestinian writers who live and work in Israel, in order to avoid a whole new set of problems. In other words, I was concerned that I might overstretch the framework that a book such as this requires.

But there are no rules without exceptions. Salman Natour is in fact a Palestinian who lives in Israel. The book needed a conclusion, a final chapter that not only summarized the content, but that could also give new perspectives, and suggest possible solutions.

For years, Natour has been actively involved in efforts to promote dialogue between the Jews and Palestinians. He has written around 25 books, and has translated several Israeli authors into Arabic. I met him in April 2002, in a lush hotel garden in East Jerusalem near the Palestinian National Theater, where he sits on the board. A smiling waiter came over to us. I suggested we have a *nargileh*, or hookah. Natour wrinkled his nose and lit up a cigarette. He ordered coffee and freshly squeezed orange juice for us both—and a hookah for me. When I later sent the Natour interview to *Klassekampen* back home in Norway, I joked that they could easily just print a picture of Gorbachev next to the article, with his birthmark airbrushed out. The likeness is striking, but Natour is gentler in both word and gesture than his Russian twin. He coughs, and exhales the cigarette smoke.

"I was born in 1949, into a war, and started school in 1956, the year of the Suez War. I finished high school in 1967 during the Six-Day War, married in 1973, the year of the Yom Kippur War. My first child was born in the middle of the 1970s, when war was raging in Lebanon; my second child was born in 1982, when Israel annihilated Beirut with bombs, and my father died during the Gulf War. My whole life is mapped out by wars. When I talk to my Israeli peers, they say, 'It's the same with me.' And I say, 'But is that a good thing? Or should we do something about it?' I'm trying to fight against all this, so that my children's lives and the lives of my grandchildren are not always described by wars."

Natour is an outspoken critic of Israel, but he also works with Jews to promote mutual understanding.

"Yes, I work actively with Jewish writers and intellectuals. I was active during the first intifada, from 1987 to 1993, alongside Habibi and Jewish authors such as Yoram Kaniuk, Nathan Zach,[2] and others. We established the Palestinian and Israeli Committee against Occupation and for Peace. I don't know whether Kaniuk told you about that? He doesn't like talking about that period. Then, during the Gulf War, we felt that the basis for continuing this work no longer existed."

"Because you were split?"

"Yes, Palestine supported Iraq and Israel supported the US, and the Israelis didn't want to meet the Palestinians anymore."

"What kind of cooperation is there today? And are you still active in this work?"

"Yes, there is cooperation between the Jews and the Palestinians, but not the Palestinians in the West Bank, only those in Israel. We now have something called the Jewish and Arab Writers' Forum, for both Arab and Jewish writers and artists who are against the occupation and war. We have activities every month in Tel Aviv and Jaffa. In fact, I was at a meeting yesterday, together with Israeli peace activists from Peace Now. And Palestinians from the West Bank do sometimes participate. I tell them that I am there with two hearts: one for the Israeli Jews and one for the Palestinians. Though obviously, these days, with all the terrible things going on in the West Bank, I am 100 percent Palestinian. I am only on the side of the victim now, and the Israelis must understand that."

He takes a deep drag on his cigarette, thinks a moment, and then clears his throat again. "But I am very glad that the meetings have continued, that the contact and dialogue with Jewish writers continues."

Tool for Peace

As this book has demonstrated, there is not much actual contact between the Palestinians and Israelis, writers or others. The political climate undoubtedly undermines any efforts to create dialogue. I ask Natour what potential he thinks literature has in this situation. And what about his own work, translating Hebrew literature into Arabic, is there a sort of mission behind that? Is it *important* for Palestinians to know about Hebrew literature?

"Extremely important. I am strongly in favor of translations, both ways. We should get to know each other better and better. Literature is a perfect way to do that, because literature allows you to have direct contact with the other side. It takes you into their society. Knowing the other side makes it possible to have dialogue. Literature is very different from the news on TV. Literature's task is to find another way in, because it cannot compete equally with television and the media. It has to start with something else, maybe a small detail, a girl's school book on the ground, something like that."

"You say that literature can help both sides to get to know each other. How far do you think this potential extends? Can literature truly be a tool for peace?"

He sits still for a moment and thinks, before looking at me again with a slow nod. "Yes, I believe it can. I believe it can."

I am interested to hear more about Natour's own translations from Hebrew to Arabic, what he has translated and why.

"I translated David Grossman's *The Yellow Wind* into Arabic in 1986, on the initiative of Mahmoud Darwish, who was living in Paris at the time and publishing the periodical *Al-Karmel* from there. Excerpts from *The Yellow Wind* were published in *Al-Karmel*, and later in three or four other Arabic periodicals. More recently I have translated two anthologies of short stories from Hebrew. I picked the authors I wanted to include: Amos Oz, A.B. Yehoshua, Etgar Keret, Orly Castel-Bloom, Amos Kenan[3] and some others."

"What were the criteria for the publications? Were you looking for political stories, for example?"

"No, I took some from the older generation and some from younger writers. Tried to give a panorama. If someone had no knowledge of Hebrew literature before, they should be able to get an idea of it by reading the anthology."

Even though Natour supports translations either way, he admits that not enough is being done. He also points out that more is translated from Hebrew into Arabic than the other way round. So, as a citizen of the state of Israel, how would he describe the Israelis' relationship to Palestinian literature? Are they interested in it?

"Not particularly, no. I recently talked to Darwish's publisher in Israel. She printed 1,000 copies of his last book, and after a year, they had only sold about 800 copies. There isn't much happening on the Hebrew to Arabic front either. But if you're asking about the Arab world as whole, it's difficult to say, because I don't read all the Arabic papers and I don't travel much to other Arab countries. Israeli Jewish writers sometimes ask me why the Arab world doesn't translate their work. I reply by asking them why they think they should. Hebrew culture and the existence of Israel is a political problem. The Arab world doesn't necessarily feel that Hebrew culture has more to offer than, say, Norwegian culture. For them, Jewish culture is just one of many. That is of course different for the Palestinians because we're so closely connected to the Israelis. But take an intellectual in Yemen, or Morocco, say, why should he know what Amos Oz writes? It is perhaps more interesting for him to know what is going on in China."

But Natour emphasizes that there is some movement; some Hebrew books do find their way into Arabic.

"A number of political writers have been published in Jordan. A couple of years ago, we established the Palestinian Center for Israeli Studies in Ramallah and translated a dozen or so academic books from Hebrew into Arabic. But it is difficult now, very difficult."

The waiter comes over with our coffee, orange juice, and the hookah. The birds chirp happily under a blue sky. But the tanks are not far away. Ramallah is only a few kilometers to the north and there is a war going on there, with a curfew. Even when I am so close, it feels unreal.

The Refugees

This is not a book about politics, certainly not in the narrowest sense. It is about identity and culture, literature and religion, dialogue and the lack of dialogue, taboos and freedom of speech. But the conflict is omnipresent. And now it is time for me to look at the political conflict in the light of all my encounters and experiences. What have I seen in the pursuit of peace?

I have been to the region twice and talked with many people— not just writers—and I can see that the Israelis clearly have set limits. Having interviewed several Israeli writers, this is what I have learned: none of the Israelis I have met are against the establishment of an independent Palestinian state, alongside Israel, with East Jerusalem as the capital. But not one of them would agree to the return of the Palestinian refugees from 1948. Around 750,000 Palestinians were forced to flee historical Palestine in 1948. If you include their descendants, that number is now obviously much higher. As I understand it, the refugee question is the most pressing unresolved issue. What does Natour think about the refugees, living as he does in Israel and knowing Israeli society from the inside?

"I know that all Israelis say that if the refugees are given the right to return, it spells the end of Israel. I'm sure that Meir Shalev and David Grossman have already told you that. *All* Israelis say that. The point is that they think like colonials. Because *they* came here and took another people's land by force, they think that the return of the Palestinians will inevitably mean that they themselves are chased out and that the Palestinians will take over the whole land. But we cannot ignore the fact that the refugees are an Israeli problem, and not a Palestinian one. The Palestinians have the right to return, this is their home and country. Everyone is of course aware of the problems connected with coming back, but that is the next step. The first step has to be that Israel recognizes this right. Then we can discuss the practical solutions with each family. Personally, I think that most of the refugees won't want to come back. But then they have to be given some kind of compensation."

I suggest that the Israelis are also worried about something else. Democracy. More than one Israeli author has given me the following argument: there is no Arab democracy, so if the Palestinian refugees come back, then one of two things will happen. Either the Jews will rule over the Palestinians, and that would be tyranny, or there would be a free and open society, and then the Palestinian majority would immediately turn the country into yet another non-democratic Arab state.

"That is also a colonial attitude. The Palestinians might be democratic. Why shouldn't we be? I'm not convinced that Israel is so very democratic."

I reply that Israeli is democratic in the sense that everyone has the right to vote and anyone can be elected to the Knesset. I ask what rights the Palestinians do not have that the Israeli Jews do.

"It is not democracy when Israel defines itself as a *Jewish* state. That is racist. Over twenty percent of the population in this country is Arab, like me. I don't want to live in a Jewish state, I want to live in a democratic state. The majority might be Jewish or Muslim, that doesn't matter to me, as long as the state is democratic. And this Jewish state has a law called 'the Law of Return,' which guarantees the right of all Jews from all over the world to come and settle here.

Whereas the Palestinians who were forced to flee in 1948, and whose houses are perhaps still standing today, are not allowed to come back. And another thing: I was born after 1948, so I have Israeli citizenship, but many of the Palestinians who live in this country and who were born before 1948 don't have that right. They are called present absentees. Is that democratic? How can Israel and Israeli authors talk about democracy? Israel should ask itself what sort of state it wants to be, one based on power or one based on justice. The Jews have the right to live here, but we Palestinians have the same right. They have created so many problems for the people here, problems that they have to solve. So no, I don't think there will ever be peace until the refugee issue is resolved."

Natour has never visited his family in Syria and Lebanon, even though he has had the opportunity to do so. Is he frightened to go there?

"No, but I don't like the regimes there. None of them are democratic. I criticize the Arab regimes in just the same way that I criticize Israel."

In April 2002, the focus of most Israelis was on the Palestinian suicide bombers. I ask him what it feels like to be a Palestinian in Israel. Does Natour feel that he is constantly being forced to defend—or at least explain—the suicide bombers to the Jewish majority in Israel?

He shakes his head and lights another cigarette. "There is no explanation. I am against it and it is not good for the Palestinian cause. At the same time I can see that there is a lack of alternatives. So what I say to the Jews in Israel is that as you don't like the suicide bombers and neither do I, could you please give the Palestinians tanks to fight with? Or airplanes, so that they can bomb Tel Aviv in the same way that you bomb Ramallah. Would that be any better? Does that make the war more understandable?"

I point out that for me it would certainly be a bit clearer if the suicide bombers targeted military installations or soldiers, not civilians.

"Of course. As you know, the settlements and military camps are heavily protected, so in this war, you have the find the weakest points. I'm very sorry to have to say it, but that's the way it is, there are no other weak points."

Political Identity

Salman Natour was born and brought up in Israel and still lives there today. I ask him about the school system for Palestinians in Israel and how a Palestinian living in Israel feels about his Palestinian identity.

Natour doesn't hesitate a moment before saying that the school system made a conscious effort to delete Palestinian history and identity. "When I grew up, there was Hebrew literature on the curriculum, and only a bit of Arabic—but certainly no Palestinian literature. They didn't speak about the Israeli Palestinians as Palestinians at all, but rather as Arabs. They thought that if I was a Palestinian, then I was Arafat. So it immediately became a political issue. The Jewish identity is very, very confused. The Palestinians don't have that problem."

"And what is the Palestinian identity?"

"A Palestinian is anyone who was born and brought up in Palestine and their descendants."

"By Palestine, you mean the historical Palestine? In other words, the British mandate?"

"Yes, the area from the Jordan River to the sea. The Palestinian identity is not an historical identity. There was no separate Palestinian identity before 1917. Nor was there a Syrian or Lebanese identity, but then the Middle East was carved up into British and French mandates."

"So in fact it is the UK and France that made these divisions."

"Yes. The UK and France created these small, national identities, or sub-identities. Before that we were Arabs, all of us. If you asked a man from Damascus what he was, he would immediately reply: 'An Arab.' Then along came the colonial powers and created differences between the Syrians and the Palestinians, etc. Personally, I don't need a Palestinian identity. For me, it's good enough to be an Arab. But because of the political conflict, I say that I am a

Palestinian. It is political, not cultural. Because in fact there is no real difference between me and an Arab from Syria or Lebanon."

"So what about Palestinian culture, in terms of those who live here in Israel, as opposed to in the West Bank or in Gaza?"

"There are no conflicts and no real cultural differences, but of course our lives are different. They live under a military occupation, and we live under a cultural occupation."

"Have the Palestinians in Israel become more like the Jews in any way?"

He thinks about this before answering. Takes a sip of his coffee and then coughs and comments with a smile on the monotone gurgling of the hookah. He says it makes him sleepy and asks if I like it. Then he calls over the waiter and asks him for more coal. He coughs again.

"No, I don't think so. But you could say that people in Israel are more modern, both Palestinians and Jews. It's more like modern Europe."

Fear

This book is in many ways about how one side sees or does not see the other. Seeing the other side physically is one aspect of this. Another is to see the other side through their literature. And yet another is how to see the other side through your own literature. How would a Palestinian author like Salman Natour describe the Palestinians' portrayal of the Jews? Unlike writers living in Ramallah, he lives inside the Israeli state and therefore in a sense is part of Israeli culture, too.

"First we have to differentiate between three different groups of Palestinian writers: Palestinians living in Israel, Palestinians living in the West Bank and Gaza, and Palestinians living abroad. As far as Palestinians in Israel are concerned, I can speak from experience. I have written about Jews myself. They are my friends, I meet them everywhere, every day. My experience of Jews is well rounded, and so I can write about how they live at home with their families, with their wives, how they love and how they hate.

Because I know. It's different for a writer living in Ramallah. He cannot write about anything other than settlers or soldiers at the checkpoints—whereas I can write a short story about myself and a Jewish friend discussing love and the universe, a writer in Ramallah couldn't even imagine that. And he doesn't need to either, because the Jew is the occupying force, and you don't write about occupying forces as anything other than occupying forces."

"Am I right in saying that the image of the Jew given by an author in the West Bank is far more one-sided than anything you might write?"

"Yes, of course. But that's because of their limited experience. For them, Jews are soldiers. They don't know any other Jews."

"How are Palestinians portrayed in Hebrew books?"

"In some cases, the Palestinian is presented as a worker, someone who serves the Jews and is weak, but generally Palestinians are portrayed as people to be feared. They talk about their fear of Palestinians. Take Yoram Kaniuk, for example, who was a young soldier in 1947–1948. He knows that Palestinians like his old neighbor in Jaffa exist somewhere out there and dream of coming back. So where does Kaniuk's humanity lie? In recognizing the Palestinians' right to be allowed to come back. But, somewhere deep inside, Kaniuk thinks that this in turn means that he can no longer stay here. For a Hebrew author, humanity toward the Palestinians inherently entails an inhumanity toward himself."

Natour holds my gaze and nods emphatically with every syllable. "This is a major and very real problem. A dilemma."

"A feeling of guilt, perhaps?"

"Yes, a thief's feeling of guilt lies deep in the Israeli psyche. Many of them know that they are guilty. The politicians and military cannot allow themselves to say or feel that they are in any way at fault, of course, but now and then a writer feels it. And they deal with this feeling in one of two ways: either they try to repress it, or they try to find a solution. Every so often, Israeli writers try to make contact and protest against the occupation. The problem is that they seldom talk about *al-Nakba* and their responsibility for what happened in 1948."

As Natour sees it, the refugee issue is at the heart of this guilt. "That is the reason why they don't want to let the 1948 refugees back, because then they will have to admit that they have been lying the whole time. Because the official version has always been that the Palestinians left their homes voluntarily. It is a psychological and moral problem."

The last piece of coal in the hookah is about to burn out and there isn't much taste left in the apple tobacco. The waiter comes over and asks if we would like anything else. Natour shrugs and asks me if I would perhaps like another smoke. I smile and shake my head. Natour orders us both another coffee. And coughs again.

"What I try to tell the Jews is that they can ask me, as a Palestinian, to help them solve their guilt problem. I don't want them, or us, to carry on suffering."

NOTES

1 Mourid Barghouti was born in 1944 in the West Bank and now lives in Cairo. He made his literary debut in 1972 and has since published a number of poetry collections. His memoirs were published in 1997 and later translated into English by Ahdaf Souief: *I Saw Ramallah* (Cairo: American University in Cairo Press, 2000).

2 The poet Nathan Zach was born in Berlin in 1930 and moved to Palestine as a child. He is recognized as one of the pioneers of the modernist movement in Hebrew poetry. He has also worked as publisher, critic, and translator.

3 Amos Kenan (born 1927 in Tel Aviv) has written novels, short stories, and plays. His best-known novel is perhaps *The Road to Ein Harod* (1984), which has been translated into seven languages, including Arabic. He is also a painter and sculptor, and has a regular column in Israel's largest newspaper, *Yediot Aharonot.*

Biographical Notes

LIANA BADR (born 1950, Jerusalem). Grew up in Jerusalem and Jericho. Her family fled to Jordan during the Six-Day War in 1967. She studied at the University of Amman and became active in the Palestinian feminist movement. Moved to Beirut after Black September (1970). Graduated in philosophy and psychology from Beirut Arab University. Worked as a journalist and helper in the Palestinian refugee camps. Moved to Damascus in 1982, and then to Tunisia in 1987. She now lives in Ramallah and works for the Ministry of Culture. She made her literary debut in 1979, and has since published novels, short stories, and a collection of poems.

ORLY CASTEL-BLOOM (born 1960, Tel Aviv). Published her first collection of short stories in 1987. Had her international breakthrough in 1992 with the novel *Dolly City*. Has studied film at the University of Tel Aviv.

MAHMOUD DARWISH (1941–2008). Darwish was born in the village of Birwe, north of Acre, which was demolished in 1948 and the whole area was incorporated into the newly established state of Israel. Darwish's family fled, but later returned and settled in another village in Israel. In 1971, Darwish went to live abroad, and from 1994 until his death split his time between Ramallah, Amman, and Paris. He was the chairman of the Palestinian Writers' Union and editor-in-chief of the literary periodical *Al-Karmel*. Darwish made his debut as a poet in 1960, but had his breakthrough in 1964 with the collection *Awraq al-zaytun* (Olive leaves) and *Ashiq min Filistin* (A lover from Palestine) in 1966. He published over 20 poetry collections and also wrote prose, including the memoir *Memory for Forgetfulness*. Darwish was regarded as Palestine's national poet and has been translated into several languages, including Hebrew.

IZZAT GHAZZAWI (1951–2003). Born and brought up on the West Bank. Studied literature in the US. He was head of the Palestinian Writers' Union, taught English literature at Birzeit University outside Ramallah, and was director of Ogarit Publishers until his death. His short stories and novels have been translated into Norwegian. He also wrote a work of nonfiction about his two years in prison in Israel. He received the Norwegian Authors' Union's Freedom of Expression Prize in 1994.

DAVID GROSSMAN (born 1954, Jerusalem). Published his first collection of short stories in 1983, and has since written several novels for both children and adults, as well as two nonfiction books about the Israeli–Palestinian conflict, and many articles (including a collection of English articles) about the conflict in the Middle East. His work has been translated into many languages, including Arabic. He studied philosophy and theater and has worked as a journalist for Israeli radio for 25 years.

YORAM KANIUK (born 1930, Tel Aviv). Lived in New York for ten years, where he worked as an artist and journalist. In 1961 he returned to Israel and made his debut as an author. He has written several novels for children and adults, short-story collections, and works of nonfiction. His work has been translated into more than twenty languages. He was a pioneering activist in the Israeli peace movement.

ETGAR KERET (born 1967, Tel Aviv). Made his debut in 1992. Extremely popular among young Israelis. He mainly writes short stories, but has also published cartoons, a children's book, a play, as well as writing a film script. The film *Skin Deep* won the Israeli "Oscar" as well as several international prizes. There are at least 50 short films based on his short stories. He teaches at the Tel Aviv University Film School. Keret has been translated into many languages, including Arabic.

SAHAR KHALIFEH (born 1941, Nablus). Published her first novel, *Lam na'vd jawari lakum* (We are not your slave girls any more), in 1974. The title demonstrates her feminist position. Her international breakthrough came in 1976 with the novel *Wild Thorns*, which has been translated into several languages, including Hebrew. As a young woman, Khalifeh entered into a traditional, arranged marriage, but divorced thirteen years later—and started to write. She has a PhD in women's studies and American literature from the University of Iowa. In addition to writing, she works on women's issues in Palestine and is director of the Women's Affairs Center in Nablus.

ZAKARIYYA MUHAMMAD (born 1951, Nablus). Studied Arabic literature at the University of Baghdad in Iraq. Moved to Jordan, where he worked as a journalist, and published his first poems in 1979 and his debut collection in 1982. He has since published three poetry collections, two novels, a collection of plays and two books about Palestinian culture. He is also a sculptor and painter.

SALMAN NATOUR (born 1949). Lives in a village on Karmel Mountain in Israel. He has written around 25 books, including short stories, plays, children's literature, a novel, and a number of works of nonfiction, including a book written in both Hebrew and Arabic about Jewish society and the relationship between the Mizrahi and Ashkenazi Jews. He has translated Hebrew literature into Arabic and worked with Jewish intellectuals for many years. Writes regularly for three Arabic newspapers: one in Haifa, one in East Jerusalem, and one in London.

AMOS OZ (born 1939, Jerusalem). Perhaps Israel's most famous (and translated) author. He published his first collection of short stories in 1965 and has since written 26 books, mostly novels, but also some collections of essays and short stories. He has been published in over 30 countries. As a fifteen year old, he rebelled against his family and moved to the Hulda kibbutz, where he lived for about 25 years, interrupted only by his military service and university. He now lives in Arad and lectures in literature at Ben-Gurion University. One of the founding members of the Peace Now movement in 1977.

DORIT RABINYAN (born in 1972, Kfar Saba). Published her first novel at the age of 22. In addition to her two novels, which have both been translated into several languages, she has also written a collection of poems and a film script. She has worked as a journalist, among other things as a film reviewer for the paper *Ma'ariv*. She has translated a Palestinian children's book into Hebrew.

MEIR SHALEV (born 1948, Nahalal). Son of the poet Itzhak Shalev. He made his debut with a children's book in 1982 and has since written books for both adults and children. He studied psychology and has produced a number of radio and television programs. He has a regular column in Israel's leading newspaper, *Yediot Aharonot*. His novels have been translated into many languages.

MAHMOUD SHUQAIR (born 1941, Sawahra near Jerusalem). Stayed in East Jerusalem after the occupation in 1967. Has been imprisoned in Israel for his political writing twice (for two years each time) and was deported immediately after the second sentence in 1975. He first lived in Lebanon and then in Amman for many years. He stayed in Prague for three years before returning to Israel in 1993. He has a PhD in philosophy and sociology. He has worked as a journalist and editor and has been the general director of the Ministry of Culture since 1994. Made his literary debut with a collection of short stories in 1975 and has since published sixteen books, including short-story collections, essays, and children's literature. Translations of some his work can be found in various anthologies and periodicals in the West.

YAHYA YAKHLIF (born 1944, Samakh). The village of Samakh by Lake Tiberias was leveled in 1948 and Yakhlif and his family were driven into exile, first in Jordan, then Beirut and Tunisia. He is connected with Fatah, for which he has worked on cultural issues for many years, both in exile and on his return to Ramallah in 1994. At the time of writing, he was the Palestinian minister of culture. Before that, he was the head of the Supreme Council of Education and Culture, a Fatah organization that works on drawing up an effective cultural policy for the future. He made his literary debut with a collection of short stories in 1972 and has since written novels and short stories.

GHASSAN ZAQTAN (born 1954, Beit Jala near Bethlehem). Lived in the al-Karama refugee camp from 1960–1967, then in Amman and Rusaifa, Jordan, where he trained as a high-school teacher. Moved to Beirut in 1979 and then to Tunisia in 1982. Published his first collection of poems in 1982 and has since published a number of poetry collections and a novel in 1995. He previously worked for the Palestinian resistance and was editor of the PLO's literary publication, *Al-Bayadir*. He now lives in Ramallah and works as a cultural journalist for the daily newspaper *Al-Ayyam*. He is also editor of the literary journal *Al-Shou'ra*.

Bibliography

The year of original publication is given in brackets. This listing aims to include all published English translations, primarily in book form, and including periodical publications when book-length editions were unavailable. Translations into Norwegian, as well as unpublished translations, are also included for those sources used in preparing this volume for which no published English translations exist.

I. Primary Literature: Israeli Writers

Castel-Bloom, Orly. *Dolly City* [1992]. Translated by Dalya Bilu. London: Loki Books, 1997.

———. *Human Parts* [2002]. Translated by Dalya Bilu. Boston: David Godine, 2003.

Grossman, David. *Be My Knife* [1998]. Translated by Vered Almog and Maya Gurantz. New York: Farrar, Straus and Giroux, 2001.

———. *The Book of Intimate Grammar* [1991]. Translated by Betsy Rosenberg. New York: Farrar, Straus and Giroux, 1994.

———. *Death as a Way of Life: Israel Ten Years after Oslo* [collection of articles]. Translated by Haim Watzman. New York: Farrar, Straus and Giroux, 2003.

———. *Duel* [1982]. Translated by Betsy Rosenberg. London: Bloomsbury, 1999.

———. *Her Body Knows* [2002]. Translated by Jessica Cohen. New York: Farrar, Straus and Giroux, 2005.

———. *Lion's Honey: The Myth of Samson* [2005]. Translated by Stuart Schoffman. Edinburgh: Canongate, 2006.

———. *See Under: Love* [1986]. Translated by Betsy Rosenberg. New York: Farrar, Straus and Giroux, 1989.

———. *Sleeping on a Wire: Conversations with Palestinians in Israel* [1992]. Translated by Haim Watzman. New York: Farrar, Straus and Giroux, 1993.

———. *The Smile of the Lamb* [1983]. Translated by Betsy Rosenberg. New York: Farrar, Straus and Giroux, 1990.

———. *Someone to Run With* [2000]. Translated by Vered Almog. New York: Farrar, Straus and Giroux, 2004.

———. *The Yellow Wind* [1987]. Translated by Haim Watzman. New York: Farrar, Straus and Giroux, 1988.

———. *The Zigzag Kid* [1994]. Translated by Betsy Rosenberg. New York: Farrar, Straus and Giroux, 2007.

Kaniuk, Yoram. *The Acrophile* [1963]. Translated by Zeva Shapiro. New York: Atheneum, 1961.

———. *Adam Resurrected* [1968]. Translated by Seymour Simckes. New York: Atheneum, 1971.

———. *Commander of the Exodus* [1999]. Translated by Seymour Simckes. New York: Grove, 2000.

———. *Confessions of a Good Arab* [1983]. Translated by Dalya Bilu. New York: George Braziller, 1988.

———. *Himmo, King of Jerusalem* [1965]. Translated by Yosef Shachter. New York: Atheneum, 1969.

———. *His Daughter* [1987]. Translated by Seymour Simckes. New York: George Braziller, 1989.

———. *The Last Jew* [1981]. Translated by Barbara Harshav. New York: Grove/Atlantic, 2006.

———. *Rockinghorse* [1974]. Translated by Richard Flantz. New York: Harper & Row, 1977.

———. *The Story of Aunt Shlomzion the Great* [1976]. Translated by Zeva Shapiro. New York: Harper & Row, 1978.

———. *Tigerhill* [1995]. Translated from the Hebrew by Kjell Risvik. Oslo: Cappelen, 1997. Not available in English.

———. *Wasserman* [1988]. Translated from the Hebrew by Kjell Risvik. Oslo: Aschehoug, 1996. Not available in English.

Keret, Etgar. *The Bus Driver Who Wanted to Be God & Other Stories.* New York: St. Martin's Press, 2001; reprint, New York: Toby Press, 2004. Includes short stories from several collections.

———. *The Girl on the Fridge: Stories.* Translated by Miriam Schlesinger and Sondra Silverston. New York: Farrar, Straus and Giroux, 2008. Includes short stories from several collections.

———. *Missing Kissinger* [1994]. Translated by Miriam Schlesinger and Sondra Silverston. New York: Vintage Books, 2008.

———. *The Nimrod Flipout* [2002]. Translated by Miriam Schlesinger and Sondra Silverston. New York: Farrar, Straus and Giroux, 2006.

Keret, Etgar, and Actus Comics. *Jetlag.* New York: Toby Press, 2005. Graphic novella adaptations of five of Keret's short stories.

Keret, Etgar, and Asaf Hanuka. *Pizzeria Kamikaze*. Gainesville: Alternative Comics, 2006. A graphic novel adaptation of Keret's story "Kneller's Happy Campers."

Keret, Etgar, and Samir el-Youssef. *Gaza Blues*. London: David Paul, 2004. A selection of short stories by Keret and by Palestinian writer el-Youssef.

Oz, Amos. *Black Box* [1987]. Translated by Nicholas de Lange. New York: Harcourt Brace Jovanovich, 1988.

——. *Don't Call It Night* [1994]. Translated by Nicholas de Lange. New York: Harcourt Brace, 1996.

——. *Elsewhere, Perhaps* [1966]. Translated by Nicholas de Lange. New York: Harcourt Brace Jovanovich, 1973.

——. *Fima* [1991]. Translated by Nicholas de Lange. New York: Harcourt Brace, 1993.

——. *In the Land of Israel* [1983]. Translated by Maurie Goldberg-Bartura. New York: Harcourt Brace Jovanovich, 1983.

——. *The Hill of Evil Counsel* [1976]. Translated by Nicholas de Lange. New York: Harcourt Brace Jovanovich, 1978.

——. *Israel, Palestine and Peace: Essays* [1994]. New York: Harcourt Brace, 1995.

——. *My Michael* [1968]. Translated by Nicholas de Lange. New York: Alfred A. Knopf, 1972.

——. *Panther in the Basement* [1995]. Translated by Nicholas de Lange. New York: Harcourt Brace, 1997.

——. *A Perfect Peace* [1982]. Translated by Hillel Halkin. New York: Harcourt Brace Jovanovich, 1985.

——. *The Same Sea* [1999]. Translated by Nicholas de Lange. New York: Harcourt Brace, 2001.

——. *The Slopes of Lebanon* [1987]. Translated by Maurie Goldberg-Bartura. New York: Harcourt Brace Jovanovich, 1989.

——. *Soumchi* [1978]. Translated by Penelope Farmer. New York: Harper & Row, 1980.

——. *The Story Begins: Essays on Literature* [1996]. New York: Harcourt Brace, 1999.

——. *A Tale of Love and Darkness* [2003]. Translated by Nicholas de Lange. New York: Harcourt Brace, 2004.

———. *To Know a Woman* [1989]. Translated by Nicholas de Lange. New York: Harcourt Brace Jovanovich, 1991.

———. *Touch the Water, Touch the Wind* [1973]. Translated by Nicholas de Lange. New York: Harcourt Brace Jovanovich, 1974.

———. *Under this Blazing Light* [1979]. Translated by Nicholas de Lange. Cambridge: Cambridge University Press, 1995.

———. *Unto Death* [1971]. Translated by Nicholas de Lange. New York: Harcourt Brace Jovanovich, 1975.

———. *Where the Jackals Howl* [1965]. Translated by Nicholas de Lange and Philip Simpson. New York: Harcourt Brace Jovanovich, 1980.

Rabinyan, Dorit. "The Exile's Return." *Guardian*, 3 April 2004.

———. *Persian Brides* [1995]. Translated by Yael Lotan. New York: George Braziller, 1998.

———. *Strand of a Thousand Pearls* [1999]. Translated by Yael Lotan. New York: Random House, 2002. Published in the United Kingdom as *Our Weddings* (London: Bloomsbury, 2001).

———. "Young, Troubled and Lost in the Promised Land." *Sunday Times* (London). December 2001.

Shalev, Meir. *The Blue Mountain* [1988]. Translated by Hillel Halkin. New York: Harper Collins, 1991.

———. *Esau* [1991]. Translated by Barbara Harshav. New York: HarperCollins, 1993.

———. *The Loves of Judith* [1994]. Translated by Barbara Harshav. New York: Ecco Press, 1999. Published in the United Kingdom as *Four Meals* (Edinburgh: Canongate, 1999). Also published under the title *As a Few Days*.

———. *My Father Always Embarrasses Me* [1998]. Chicago: Wellington, 1991.

———. *A Pigeon and a Boy* [2006]. Translated by Evan Fallenberg. New York: Schocken, 2007.

II. Primary Literature: Palestinian Writers

Badr, Liana. *A Balcony over the Fakihani* [1983] [as Liyana Badr]. Translated by Peter Clark with Christopher Tingley. Northampton: Interlink Books, 1993.

―――. *A Compass for the Sunflower* [1979]. Translated by C. Cobham. London: the Women's Press, 1989.

―――. *The Eye of the Mirror* [1994]. Translated by Samira Kawar. Reading: Garnet, 1994.

―――. "The Trellised Vine" [no date]. *A Land of Stone and Thyme: An Anthology of Palestinian Short Stories.* Edited by Nur and Abdelwahab Elmessiri. London: Quartet Books, 1996.

Darwish, Mahmoud. *The Adam of Two Edens: Selected Poems by Mahmoud Darwish* [1990–1995]. Edited by Munir Akash and Daniel Moore. Syracuse: Syracuse University Press, 2000. A selection of poems from three collections published in 1990, 1992, and 1995.

―――. *The Butterfly's Burden.* Translated by Fady Joudah. Port Townsend: Copper Canyon Press, 2007. Includes poems from several collections.

―――. *Memory for Forgetfulness: August, Beirut, 1982* [1987]. Translated by Ibrahim Muzzawi. Berkeley: University of California Press, 1995.

―――. *The Music of Human Flesh: Poems of the Palestinian Struggle.* Translated by Denys Johnson-Davies. Washington, DC: Three Continents Press, 1980. A selection of poems from seven collections.

―――. *Psalms.* Translated by Ben Bennani. Washington, DC: Three Continents Press, 1994.

―――. "Palestine: The Imaginary and the Real." Translated by Dr. Abdul-Fattah Jabr. *Innovation in Palestinian Literature: Testimonies of Palestinian Poets and Writers.* Revised by Robert Thompson and Izzat Ghazzawi. Ramallah: Ogarit, 2000.

―――. "Poem of the Land" (and other undated poems). *Anthology of Modern Palestinian Literature.* Edited and introduced by Salma Khadra Jayyusi. New York: Columbia University Press, 1992.

―――. *The Raven's Ink: A Chapbook.* Translated and edited by Munir Akash, Carolyn Forché, Amira al-Zein, and Sinan

Antoon. The Lannan Foundation, 2001. Includes poems from several collections.

———. "Rita and the Rifle," "The Sparrows Die in Galilee," and "The Sleeping Garden." In Abdullah al-Shahham, "A Portrait of the Israeli Woman as the Beloved: The Woman-Soldier in the Poetry of Mahmud Darwish after the 1967 War." *Bulletin* (British Society for Middle Eastern Studies) 15.1–2 (1988): 28–49.

———. *Selected Poems.* Translated by Ian Wedde and Fawwaz Tuqan. Manchester: Carcanet Press, 1973.

———. *Unfortunately, It was Paradise: Selected Poems.* Translated and edited by Munir Akash and Carolyn Forché, with Sinan Antoon and Amira al-Zein. Berkeley: University of California Press, 2003.

———. *Why Did You Leave the Horse Alone?* [1995]. Translated by Jeffrey Sacks. New York: Archipelago, 2006.

Ghazzawi, Izzat. *Brev underveis: Palestinske brev fra israelske fengsler* [1991] [Letters underway: Palestinian letters from Israeli prisons]. Translated from the Arabic by Anne Aabakken. Oslo: Cappelen, 1994. Not available in English.

———. *Footsteps.* Translated by the author. Edited by Robert Bryan Thompson. Ramallah: Ogarit Cultural Center, 2002.

———. *Nebo-fjellet* [1995] [Nebo Mountain]. Translated from the Arabic by Anne Aabakken. Oslo: Cappelen, 1997. Only an excerpt available in English: "Nebo Mountain." Translator unknown. *Palestine–Israel Journal* 12.4 and 13.1 (2005/2006).

———. *Sannheten sover* [2002] [The truth sleeps]. Translated from the Arabic by Anne Aabakken. Oslo: Cappelen, 2004. Not available in English.

Khalifeh, Sahar. *The End of Spring.* Translated by Paula Haydar. Northampton: Interlink Books, 2007.

———. *The Image, the Icon, and the Covenant.* Translated by Aida Bamia. Northampton: Interlink Books, 2007.

———. *The Inheritance.* Translated by Aida Bamia. New York: American University in Cairo Press, 2005.

———. *Memoirs of an Unrealistic Woman* [1986]. Extract from this novel in *Anthology of Modern Palestinian Literature.* Edited and introduced by Salma Khadra Jayyusi. New York: Columbia University Press, 1992.

————."My Life, Myself, and the World." *Al-Jadid* 8.39 (2002).

————. *Wild Thorns* [1976]. Translated by Trevor Legassick and Elizabeth Fernea. Northampton: Interlink Books, 1985.

Muhammad, Zakariyya. "Apology" (and other undated poems). *Anthology of Modern Palestinian Literature.* Edited and introduced by Salma Khadra Jayyusi. New York: Columbia University Press, 1992.

————. "Caravan" (and other undated poems). *Modern Palestinian Poetry in Translation.* Edited by Izzat Ghazzawi. Jerusalem: The Palestinian Writers' Union, 1997.

Natour, Salman. "A Break." Translated by Yasir Suleiman. *Banipal* 15/16 (2002–2003): 84–86.

————. "Memory." *Innovation in Palestinian Literature: Testimonies of Palestinian Poets and Writers.* Revised by Robert Thompson and Izzat Ghazzawi. Ramallah: Ogarit, 2000.

Shuqair, Mahmoud. "The Homeland" [1975]. *A Land of Stone and Thyme: An Anthology of Palestinian Short Stories.* Edited by Nur and Abdelwahab Elmessiri. London: Quartet Books, 1996.

————. "Seven Short Stories." *Modern Palestinian Short Stories in Translation.* Edited by Izzat Ghazzawi and Claire Peak. Jerusalem: The Palestinian Writers' Union, 1998.

————. "Shakira's Picture" and "Ronaldo's Seat" [2003]. Translated by Diana Khouri. Unpublished.

————. "Un autre café," "Fragments," and "Laine" [1999]. *Revue d'etudes Palestiniennes* 24 (2000).

————. "The Villagers" [1963]. *Anthology of Modern Palestinian Literature.* Edited and introduced by Salma Khadra Jayyusi. New York: Columbia University Press, 1992.

Yakhlif, Yahya. *A Lake Beyond the Wind* [1991]. Translated by May Jayyusi and Christopher Tingley. Northampton: Interlink Books, 1999.

————. "Desert Island, Lost Lake: Excerpt from a Play." Translated by Leila Dabdoub. *Palestine–Israel Journal* 3.2 (1996).

————. "The Lost Birds." *Modern Palestinian Short Stories in Translation.* Edited by Izzat Ghazzawi and Claire Peak. Jerusalem: The Palestinian Writers' Union, 1998.

————. "Norma and the Snowman." *A Land of Stone and Thyme: An Anthology of Palestinian Short Stories.* Edited by Nur and

Abdelwahab Elmessiri. London: Quartet Books, 1996.

———. "That Rose of a Woman" [1981]. *Anthology of Modern Palestinian Literature.* Edited and introduced by Salma Khadra Jayyusi. New York: Columbia University Press, 1992.

Zaqtan, Ghassan. "Alone and the River Before Me." Translated by Fady Joudah. *Modern Poetry in Translation* 3.9. Issue edited by David and Helen Constantine.

———. "Another Death" (and other undated poems). *Anthology of Modern Palestinian Literature.* Edited and introduced by Salma Khadra Jayyusi. New York: Columbia University Press, 1992.

———. "Beirut, August 1982." Translated by Sarah Maguire with Kate Daniels. *100 Poets Against The War.* Edited by Todd Swift. Cambridge: Salt Publishing, 2003.

———. "Darkness" (and other undated poems). Translated by Sarah Maguire with Kate Daniels. *Banipal* 15/16 (2002–2003): 148–150.

———. "An Exit" (and other undated poems). *Modern Palestinian Poetry in Translation.* Edited by Izzat Ghazzawi. Jerusalem: The Palestinian Writers' Union, 1997.

———. "Guide" (and other undated poems). *Banipal* 12 (Fall 2001).

———. "The Image of the House in Bait Jala," "Old Passages," "Revisions," and "He Was Not Asleep" [no date]. *Virginia Quarterly Review* 84.3 (summer 2008).

———. *Du tok fatt i meg og forsvant/* [You took hold of me and disappeared]. Translated from the Arabic by Ulla Stang Dahl. Oslo: Oktober, 2003. A collection of poems published between 1982 and 1999. Not available in English.

III. Secondary Literature

I have not included book reviews here, even though I have read a great many reviews of Palestinian and Israeli books over the past few years. I have gained much insight and enjoyment from the excellent publication *World Literature Today* and also the *Times Literary Supplement, London Review of Books,* and *New York Times Book Review,* not to mention the Friday edition of the English version of the Israeli newspaper *Haaretz:* www.haaretzdaily.com.

English

Abdel-Malek, Kamal, and David C. Jacobson, eds. *Israeli and Palestinian Identities in History and Literature.* New York: St. Martin's Press, 1999.

Alcalay, Ammiel. "Who's Afraid of Mahmoud Darwish?" *Middle East Report* 154 (1988): 27–28.

al-Shahham, Abdullah. "A Portrait of the Israeli Woman as the Beloved: The Woman Soldier in the Poetry of Mahmud Darwish after the 1967 War." *Bulletin* (British Society for Middle Eastern Studies) 15.1–2 (1988): 28–49.

Boullata, Issa J. "An Arabic Poem in an Israeli Controversy: Mahmud Darwish's 'Passing Words.'" *Humanism, Culture and Language in the Near East: Studies in Honor of Georg Krotkoff.* Edited by Afsar Uddin and A.H. Mathias Zahniser. Winona Lake: Eisenbrauns, 1997.

Elad-Bouskila, Ami. *Modern Palestinian Literature and Culture.* London: Frank Cass, 1999.

Hafez, Sabry. "The Novel, Politics and Islam: Haydar Haydar's Banquet for Seaweed." *New Left Review* 5 (2000).

Jayyusi, Salma Khadra. "Introduction: Palestinian Literature in Modern Times." *Anthology of Modern Palestinian Literature.* Edited by Salma Khadra Jayyusi. New York: Columbia University Press, 1992.

Johnson-Davies, Denys. "Introduction." *The Music of Human Flesh: Poems of the Palestinian Struggle.* By Mahmoud Darwish. London: Heinemann, 1980.

Majaj, Lisa Suhair, Paula W. Sunderman, and Theresa Saliba, eds. *Intersections: Gender, Nation and Community in Arab Women's Novels.* Syracuse: Syracuse University Press, 2002.

Matta, Nada. "Postcolonial Theory, Multiculturalism and the Israeli Left: a Critique of Post-Zionism." *Holy Land Studies* 2.1 (2003).

Moreh, Shmuel. "The Study of Arabic Literature in Israel." *Ariel* 112 (2001): 66–73.

Naim, Mona. "'My Opposition to the Terms of the Accord is a Measure of my Attachment to Real Peace.'" Interview with Mahmoud Darwish. *Middle East Report* May–June/July–August 1995. Originally printed in the French *Le Monde* 12–13 March 1995.

Negev, Eilat. *Close Encounters with Twenty Israeli Writers.* London: Valentine Mitchell, 2003.

"Poetry Sends Israel into a Political Storm." *BBC News* online, 7 July 2000 <News.bbc.co.uk/1/hi/world/middle_east/668702.stm>.

Shehadeh, Raja. *When the Birds Stopped Singing: Life in Ramallah Under Siege.* Hanover: Steerforth, 2003.

Taha, Ibrahim. *The Palestinian Novel: A Communication Study.* London: Routledge/Curzon, 2002.

Zeidan, Joseph T. *Arab Women Novelists: The Formative Years and Beyond.* Albany: State University of New York Press, 1995.

Norwegian

Abu Matar, Ahmed. "Bildet av jøden i palistinske romaner." *Materialisten* 2/3 (1997).

Borge, Torunn. "Hymne til de knuste glass. En introduksjon til Ghassan Zaqtans poesi." *Vinduet* 1–2 (2002).

Isaksen, Runo. www.runo.no [Interviews with Israeli and Palestinian authors, originally published in *Klassekampen* spring 2002 and autumn 2003, and an in-depth interview published in *Morgenbladet* 50 (12–18 December 2003). Also includes reviews of several Israeli and Palestinian authors, published in *Klassekampen*.]

Isaksen, Runo. "Et perfekt bru" [about Dorit Rabinyan]. *Syn og Segn* 3 (2004).

Morken, Johannes. "I skuggen av eit statsministerdrap." Interview with David Grossman. *Idé* 3–4 (1995): 22–26.

Morken, Johannes. "Vismannen frå Oz." Interview with Amos Oz. *Idé* 3–4 (1993).

Steien, Solveig. "Fedre og sønner." Interview with Izzat Ghazzawi. *Forfatteren* 4 (1994).